THE CONSULTANT'S GUIDE TO LITIGATION SERVICES

HOW TO BE AN EXPERT WITNESS

THOMAS H. VEITCH

John Wiley & Sons, Inc.
New York • Chichester • Brisbane • Toronto • Singapore

In recognition of the importance of preserving what has been written, it is a policy of John Wiley & Sons, Inc., to have books of enduring value published in the United States printed on acid-free paper, and we exert our best efforts to that end.

Published by John Wiley & Sons, Inc.

Library of Congress Cataloging-in-Publication Data:

Veitch, Thomas H., 1938–
The consultant's guide to litigation services : how to be an expert witness / Thomas H. Veitch.
p. cm.
Includes index.
ISBN 0-471-55406-5
1. Evidence, Expert—United States. 2. Examination of witnesses—United States. I. Title.
KF8961.V45 1992
347.73'6—dc20
[347.3076] 92-14945

Printed in the United States of America

10 9 8 7 6 5 4 3 2 1

Preface

As cases facing litigation have become increasingly complex in recent years, the judicial system's reliance on expert testimony has increased markedly. Indeed, the opinion of findings of an expert may be indispensable in establishing the possible negligence of a professional, the faulty design of a piece of machinery, or the damages for a particular case. Carol Stein of the Technical Advisory Service for Attorneys (TASA), a major expert witness brokerage firm, estimates that 90 percent of cases settled or brought to trial in the United States involve some expert opinion. And there are as many types of experts as there are types of cases. TASA, alone, provides specialists in more than 4,000 categories. And while experts are becoming omnipresent on the witness stand, there is also a broader trend toward "litigation consulting" by specialists behind the scenes. Consultants and specialists of all kinds are working closely with attorneys on strategy and tactics.

There are few greater challenges for the expert than facing an astute attorney whose job it is to grind down or destroy that expert's credibility under cross-examination. Thorough preparation is necessary for the often intense, and sometimes perilous, questioning and probing. In addition, the expert should have a strong command of the vocabulary and processes of the judicial system and legal profession to avoid inadvertently becoming impaled on a technicality or misunderstood procedure. Although the challenge is indeed great, the properly prepared specialist can be confident that his or her opinions and statements will "stand up" in court.

This book has been written to provide just this kind of preparation. It can be used by experts in any field as a primer on the litigation process in general, and the expert's role in particular. I have provided an abundance of real-life examples throughout this volume, to make it as practical and useful as possible. In addition, I have excerpted verbatim the most crucial portions of the federal rules governing judicial procedure that apply to expert testimony; I have summarized the more tangential rules. These rules form the almost universal basis for lower courts' procedures.

I hope that readers will find the "Key Words and Phrases" sections helpful. Since the terms in these sections are listed at the end of the chapter in which they are discussed, readers are encouraged to use the Index to locate definitions throughout the book. I also hope readers will benefit from the "Practice Tips" in this book, which encompass many "unspoken rules" that can trip up the first-time expert witness.

I wish you every success in serving the judicial system with your expertise.

THOMAS H. VEITCH

San Antonio, Texas

Contents

CHAPTER 1

Introduction to the Courtroom Scene

You may be considering whether to become an **expert witness.*** Or perhaps you are an experienced consultant looking for ways to be better prepared for the arduous experience of consulting and testifying in a lawsuit. Possibly you are a layperson and simply want to know more about this area of the law in case you ever need to testify as a witness (e.g., as an eyewitness to an automobile accident).

Most people are intimidated by the litigation process and its exposure to, or confrontations with, often boisterous or stern lawyers, judges, and other courtroom players. This is especially true if you have had no prior experience, or worse yet, have had one or two unfavorable past experiences.

THE BASICS

This book will enable you to better understand the litigation process and what is expected of witnesses. While the comments and

*Key items appear in boldface and are defined in the Glossary at the end of each chapter.

ideas expressed herein are designed primarily for consultants or expert witnesses, much of the material will also be helpful to any person who is expecting to appear as a witness in a legal matter. This first chapter introduces you to the legal process so that you will have a general knowledge of how it all fits together. The greater your understanding, the more quickly you will develop confidence and feel comfortable with the legal process.

The middle chapters focus on the role of the expert, marketing your practice, setting fees, doing your homework, and other professional matters.

The final chapters contain extensive material to illustrate the procedures, perils, and pitfalls of depositions, direct examination, and cross-examination, and how to deal with them. In short, this book will explain the litigation process, provide valuable information for building a professional practice, and illustrate what to expect when you testify (and how to perform successfully).

Expert Witnesses versus Lay Witnesses

All witnesses in a lawsuit, whether they are experts or simply lay witnesses, are exposed to the uncertainties of a deposition and the rigors of direct and cross-examination. Simply stated, a **lay witness** is a nonprofessional witness; the classification also includes parties to a lawsuit. For example, if you are involved in an automobile accident while driving your vehicle and a lawsuit ensues, you will undoubtedly be required to testify, as a lay witness, if the case goes to trial. Any doctors, police officers, accident reconstructionists, or other professionals who testify in the case, however, would be expert witnesses.

The Litigation Process—Civil versus Criminal Courts

Civil actions are concerned with private rights and remedies as contrasted with criminal law, which pertains to actions violating laws that govern human conduct and prevent harm to society.

Automobile accidents, workers' compensation cases, business disputes, suits on a contract, divorce, and bankruptcy are all examples of civil suits. In most states, criminal courts and civil courts are segregated from one another. Although expert witnesses frequently testify in criminal matters, the major opportunities for independent witnesses are in civil cases. Most civil cases of any magnitude require the assistance and possible testimony of expert witnesses to meet the burdens of proof required in the case. Accordingly, this material focuses primarily on experts in civil cases although it will be useful in criminal cases as well.

THE DEVELOPMENT OF A LAWSUIT

Without lawsuits, the need for expert witnesses quickly vanishes. Accordingly, it is important to understand the genesis of the litigation process and how a lawsuit actually develops. Before a lawsuit is filed, some occurrence must generate a dispute. A defective product causes severe injury to a worker, a husband and wife decide to divorce, a pedestrian is struck by a hit-and-run driver, a dispute arises over the ownership of a large tract of land, business partners have a falling out, or some similar event provokes a dispute between two or more parties. When this happens and the parties cannot readily resolve their differences, one of them will inevitably seek legal advice to determine what can be done about the problem. Of course, the mere existence of a dispute does not necessarily mean that litigation will result. In most cases, this will depend on the advice and counsel the injured party receives as a result of contacting a lawyer.

Investigation

Prior to accepting a case or advising that there is a basis for legal recovery, most responsible lawyers will conduct some investigations of the pertinent facts and issues. In many instances, the basic investigation may require the counsel or assistance of an expert witness. For example, if the case concerns a defective product, there must be an initial determination as to what happened and who may be implicated. Complex products contain many intricate parts that may involve a variety of manufacturers or distributors. The immediate opinion of an expert may be necessary "to sort the wheat from the chaff" and to determine whether a meritorious case exists and who are the potentially responsible parties. The investigation may also explore the financial solvency or stability of proposed target defendants or the applicability of insurance coverage.

Whether or not an expert is consulted at this juncture, some basic investigation is necessary to determine the facts of the case.

Theory of the Case

The facts and information gathered at the outset of a case will be utilized to evaluate the merits of the potential case, determine the legal theories on which the case will be based, and to establish appropriate jurisdiction and **venue**.

For example, if the litigation concerns a vehicular accident in which a truck driver ran a red light and crashed into a passenger car occupied by a mother and two children causing severe injuries to all, some immediate questions arise:

1. Who owns the truck?
2. Who was the truck driver working for?
3. Was the truck driver engaged in the scope of his employment when the accident occurred?
4. Why did the truck driver run the red light?
5. Were the occupants of the passenger vehicle wearing safety belts?
6. Did the safety equipment function properly?
7. Did the passenger vehicle withstand the impact in a reasonable and expected manner?

8. What insurance coverages are applicable?
9. What is the extent of damages in relation to the applicable insurance coverage?
10. What other factors, if any, caused or contributed to the cause of the accident or the damages sustained therein?

The answers to these and other pertinent inquiries shape the theory of the case and determine how it will be developed for settlement or, if an out-of-court settlement is not feasible, how it will be litigated.

Pleadings in Civil Cases

A lawsuit is commenced by preparing and filing a complaint or petition outlining the plaintiff's complaints, allegations, and theories of recovery against the defendant or defendants. The defendants in turn file an answer or response stating their defenses or general position in the case. In other words, the **pleadings** are the written allegations of the respective parties to the litigation and form the basis of the dispute to be resolved by the litigation process. The purpose of the pleadings is to provide fair notice of the claims being made and apprise the parties of their respective positions and contentions.

Witnesses and Other Evidence

While the pleadings frame the initial issues and positions of the parties, the outcome of the case will depend on the **evidence** presented. The "trier of the facts" will be either the judge or a jury, who will decide the case based on that evidence.

Oral testimony will be provided by the witnesses. This testimony may be presented live in the courtroom or by deposition. The deposition testimony in many cases may be by videotape presentation if the case warrants this expenditure and effort. Sometimes written deposition testimony will be read aloud in the courtroom to the court or jury. This can be somewhat boring to a judge or jury, so a live witness presentation is generally preferable. Even the best of evidence can be worthless to a "sleeping juror." The physical procedure for presenting evidence by witness testimony is basically the same whether the witness is an expert or a lay witness. However, the legal procedure may vary depending on the **jurisdiction**. Generally, a much broader latitude is given to the questions that can be asked of an expert, while lay witness testimony will usually be confined to the facts within the witness's knowledge. An expert is permitted to testify as to his or her opinions based on hypothetical facts and circumstances.

In addition to the evidence presented by the live or deposition testimony of witnesses, the following forms of evidence are frequently utilized:

1. Documentary evidence.
2. Books and records.
3. Film or recordings.
4. Test results.
5. Written reports.

Often, expert witnesses are used to prepare or analyze some of these other forms of evidence and explain them to the judge and jury.

THE PRINCIPAL PLAYERS

In civil cases, the **plaintiffs** and defendants occupy the leading roles. The plaintiff initiates the action by filing a complaint against the applicable defendant or defendants. A civil lawsuit may have one or several plaintiffs and defendants depending on the nature of the case.

The Supporting Cast

The courtroom drama is completed with a variety of role players.

The attorneys are officers of the court and serve as advocates for the positions to be promoted by their respective clients, the plaintiffs and the defendants. For the most part, the attorneys control the tempo of the drama as they select the jury, present the evidence, and argue their case.

The judge has ultimate control over the attorneys' conduct, the admissibility of evidence, and the general flow of the trial.

The court clerk assists the judge on clerical matters and administers the oath to the jurors and testifying witnesses. In many courts, the clerk does not sit in the courtroom for the entire trial, but is generally available to assist the judge as required.

On the other hand, the bailiff and court reporter will be present for the entire trial. The bailiff is charged with maintaining order and decorum in the courtroom. The bailiff also assures the security and safety of all present and assists the judge with various matters such as the summoning of witnesses into the courtroom and the supervision of jurors.

The court reporter records all the testimony of witnesses in the case as well as any other pertinent courtroom proceeding such as jury selection, opening statements, oral motions of counsel, bench conferences with the judge and attorneys, and the closing argument of counsel. The court reporter is also responsible for marking exhibits for evidence and assuring that all such exhibits are intact and in order for the jury to consider when the attorneys have completed the presentation of their cases.

The Jury

Occasionally the parties to a civil case will waive a jury for tactical or economic reasons, and in some instances, the law of the jurisdiction may not allow for a jury. However, most civil lawsuits and virtually all criminal cases are tried by a jury.

The jury possesses the power to determine the outcome of the case. Accordingly, a great deal of established trial procedure as well as the efforts and tactics of the attorneys are directed toward the selection and shaping of the jury and its ultimate decisions.

The decisions of the jury are based on the facts of the case, and juries are referred to as "the trier of the facts." Even in jury cases, all issues of law are retained by the judge. In nonjury trials, the judge becomes the trier of the facts as well as the authority on the law of the case.

Attorneys consider the jury selection process to be a crucial part of the case. Since it is the first step in the actual trial of the case, it sets the mood for the entire trial. It provides the opportunity to determine which persons will serve on the jury and allows the attorney to focus the attention of the potential jurors on significant aspects of the case. This is all accomplished by the **voir dire** process, which is discussed later in this chapter. The jury will be guided in its deliberations by the court's instructions and the issues submitted to them in the case.

TYPES OF COURTS

To understand the intricacies of the litigation process, it is helpful to have some understanding of the different types of courts and their jurisdiction or purpose. In some states, the same courts may handle both criminal and civil cases, while in others, the civil and criminal courts may be separate and apart from one another even though they may legally possess both civil and criminal jurisdiction. The primary distinction is between federal and state courts. Civil and criminal matters are adjudicated within both these systems. Additionally, both systems provide for an appellate process.

State Courts

Although there may be some distinctions between courts of civil and criminal jurisdiction, particularly as to rules of evidence and procedure, they can be considered for our purposes to be virtually the same. Generally speaking, a state court system will consist of the following courts in ascending order.

Justice Courts and Municipal Courts. These are courts of inferior or limited jurisdiction. Frequently they are not courts of record. They may be the primary court for specified matters such as traffic tickets, violation of city ordinances, or eviction cases, but they usually have very limited jurisdiction on other matters, if any at all.

County Courts. These are courts of record and usually have **concurrent jurisdiction** with state district courts on most negligence and contract cases or related civil matters up to a specified dollar amount (e.g., $50,000 in Texas). Relative to criminal matters, county courts may be limited to misdemeanor cases while felony cases are the responsibility of state district courts.

State District Courts. These courts have general original jurisdiction for all civil matters within a specified judicial district. Most metropolitan areas will have several state district courts and probably a number of county courts as well. Therefore, you must know the number of the court to which a case has been assigned to determine where you need to appear (e.g., 250th District Court or County Court No. 6).

Courts of Special Jurisdiction. Many states have special courts to handle divorce cases, probate, juvenile cases, or similar specialized matters. This varies by state and usually is limited to metropolitan areas. In rural areas, the courts are required to deal with a greater diversity of cases.

Court of Appeals. The court of appeals is both a court of law and a court of equity and consists of a chief justice and several associate justices. If the court is large, usually a panel of three or more justices will be assigned to a case rather than the entire court being required to hear each appeal. Most states have separate appellate courts for criminal and civil jurisdiction. Therefore, a civil court of appeals hears only civil cases, and criminal cases go before a court of criminal appeals.

Supreme Court. As the name implies, and like the federal court system, this is usually the court of highest jurisdiction. Cases that are not finally resolved at the trial court or court of appeals level may ascend to the state supreme court. While most cases reaching the supreme court level are resolved by a final decision, many are remanded back to the trial court for final resolution in accordance with guidelines enunciated by the supreme court. Final decisions of the supreme court are controlling precedent for future cases on related issues of law.

Federal Courts

It is important to remember that the federal courts are housed separately from state courts. In some instances, the federal courthouse may be located a considerable distance from the state courthouse. From the standpoint of the witness, knowing which courthouse you need to locate is the primary distinction between the two court systems. Although there are differences in procedure and formalities, none of them particularly alter the role and function of the expert witness.

In general, the federal court system consists of the following courts.

Federal District Court. The district court is the primary federal court for most civil cases requiring expert witnesses. The federal district court also handles minor criminal cases and immigration matters.

Often there is concurrent jurisdiction between state and federal courts, which allows attorneys to choose the court that they want to litigate the case. This often results in the use of the removal procedure, whereby a case filed in a state court might be removed to a federal court for litigation or vice versa. Whether or not a federal court has jurisdiction of a matter depends on (1) the nature of the parties to the action, (2) the nature of the issues involved, or (3) possibly both.

United States Magistrate Court. This court has federal jurisdiction of most misdemeanor cases and performs specified duties delegated by federal district courts. The **magistrate** courts may also serve as **special master** in specialized civil cases.

Courts of Special Jurisdiction. There are several specialized federal courts, all of which have their own special rules and procedures. Examples are the tax court, customs court, bankruptcy court, and court of claims.

Courts of Appellate Jurisdiction. The United States Court of Appeals for the federal circuit serves as the primary **appellate jurisdiction** followed by the United States Supreme Court. However, the United States Supreme Court does have original jurisdiction in certain specified matters. Also, in some instances appeals can be made directly from a federal district court to the United States Supreme Court.

TRIAL DISCOVERY

Discovery is the process of marshaling the appropriate evidence to prepare a case for trial. By utilizing various discovery methods, the attorneys are able to acquire a vast amount of information regarding the facts in the case. Although much of what is acquired may not be used or even may not be **admissible evidence**, the facts do form a knowledge pool with which the attorneys can evaluate the merits of their case and the respective positions of the parties. By the time the plaintiffs commence a lawsuit with the filing of original pleadings, both sides will presumably have conducted some preliminary investigation. At this juncture, however, each side lacks much of the documentation and records possessed by the other. Additionally, they do not know with any precision who the opponents' witnesses will be or what they will say. In reality, it often takes the formalities of trial preparation for the parties really to focus on their respective positions and the details supporting such a position.

The rules of evidence and rules of procedure in the various state jurisdictions and the federal rules provide the guidelines by which such discovery is conducted.

Scope of Discovery

The trend during the past several years has been to broaden the scope of what is or is not discoverable. The rules specify what may be properly obtained and what is subject to confidentiality or privilege. There is some variance in the rules from state to state as well as between the state and federal rules. The trend, however, seems to be for state rules to be substantially in conformity with the federal rules.

Because of the importance of obtaining access to vital documents or information, there is often substantial disagreement between or among opposing counsel as to what is, and is not, discoverable under the applicable rules. Such disagreements are a basic part of the "jockeying for position" and "tactical maneuvering" involved in preparing a case for trial. Once a case is actually prepared and set for trial, some of the disagreements developed in the trial discovery process will carry over into the trial proceedings for determinations by the court as to what is proper or what constitutes admissible evidence. It should be noted that the purpose of discovery is to enable the parties to get at the truth so that disputes can be resolved by what the facts reveal. Accordingly, courts tend to liberalize this "fact hunting expedition" as much as possible.

This is illustrated by the following excerpt from Rule 26 of the Federal Rules of Civil Procedure:

> Parties may obtain discovery regarding any matter, not privileged, which is relevant to the subject matter involved in the pending action, whether it relates to the claim or defense of the party seeking discovery or the claim or defense of any other party, including the existence, description, nature, custody, condition and location of any books, documents, or other tangible things and the identity and location of persons having knowledge of any discoverable matter. *It is not ground for objection that the information sought will be inadmissible at the trial if the information sought appears reasonably calculated to lead to the discovery of admissible evidence* [emphasis added].

However, the rules are nonetheless designed to be protective where necessary, so that so-called fact hunting expeditions are not merely fishing expeditions. For example, Rule 26(C) Protective Orders (Federal Rules of Civil Procedure), allows a party to file a motion with the court for any order that justice requires, to protect a party or person from annoyance, embarrassment, oppression, or undue burden or expense.

Discovery Methods

The parameters for trial discovery are set forth in Rule 26(a) Discovery Methods (Federal Rules of Civil Procedure) as follows:

> (a) Discovery Methods. Parties may obtain discovery by one or more of the following methods: depositions upon oral examination or written questions; written interrogatories; production of documents or things or permission to enter upon land or other property, for inspection and other purposes physical and mental examinations; and requests for admission.

The discovery methods provided for in this rule are essentially the same as those provided for and utilized in all state jurisdictions.

Oral Depositions and Depositions on Written Questions. **Depositions**, particularly oral depositions, are the principally used discovery method for trial purposes. As an expert witness, you can count on being deposed in each and every case that is being prepared for trial. Occasionally a case may be settled before a designated expert's deposition is obtained, but more frequently the depositions of the experts are likely to be the "ammunition" that motivates peace rather than war. See Chapter 5 for a more extensive discussion of the deposition procedure.

Written Interrogatories. The use of **interrogatories** is limited to the parties in the case, whereas depositions may be taken of lay witnesses, expert witnesses, and other nonparties. Interrogatories are propounded in the form of written questions that must be answered in writing by the parties upon which they are served. Rule 33 of the Federal Rules of Civil Procedure provides the criteria for the use of interrogatories. The key points in Rule 33 may be summarized as follows:

1. Interrogatories may be served only on parties.
2. If the party served is a business or governmental entity, then an authorized officer or agent must furnish all such information in responding as is possessed by the party collectively, not just of the person preparing the response.
3. All answers are provided separately in writing, and under oath.
4. Answers, and objections if any, are due within 30 days after the interrogatory is served.
5. The time for response may be lengthened or shortened by the court.

As a general rule, interrogatories are one of the first items of discovery advanced to elicit general information preliminary to depositions and other discovery. It is usually difficult to pin down any key facts by this method.

> ***Practice Tip:*** **Interrogatories and their responses frequently need to be reviewed by expert witnesses relative to basic facts in the case.**

Production of Documents or Things. This discovery method is useful for several reasons. First, it gains access to tangible evidence in the possession of an opposing party. Second, tangible evidence, such as actual documents or other physical items, can be convincing evidence to jurors and is often more persuasive than mere verbal comments. Finally, a review of pertinent documents and records often leads to key items of evidence or potential trial strategy.

The scope of this method is reflected by Rule 34 of the Federal Rules of Civil Procedure:

> RULE 34. PRODUCTION OF DOCUMENTS AND THINGS AND ENTRY UPON LAND FOR INSPECTION AND OTHER PURPOSES
> (a) Scope. Any party may serve on any other party a request (1) to produce and permit the party making the request, or someone acting on the requestor's behalf, to inspect and copy, any designated documents (including writings, drawings, graphs, charts, photographs, phono-records, and other data compilations from which information can be obtained, translated, if necessary, by the respondent through detection devices into reasonably usable form), or to inspect and copy, test, or sample any tangible things which constitute or contain matters within the scope of Rule 26(b) and which are in the possession, custody or control of the party upon whom the request is served; or (2) to permit entry upon designated land or other property in the possession or control of the party upon whom the request is served for the purpose of inspection and measuring, surveying, photographing, testing, or sampling the property or any designated object or operation thereon, within the scope of Rule 26(b).

Requests for Admission. This method may effectively limit the issues in controversy by seeking the admission of either party of the truth of a particular matter. In addition, responses to admissions often pinpoint problem areas or key issues. For this reason, a **request for admissions** may help the expert witness gain a basic grasp of the case being reviewed.

Rule 36 of the Federal Rules of Civil Procedure sets forth the guidelines for their use and may be summarized as follows:

1. They may be served only on parties to the case (not witnesses).
2. They must be submitted in writing.
3. Requests for admission pertain only to the case in which they are submitted, not collateral matters.
4. This is a very useful method for proving the genuineness of documents. For example, an attorney might ask a plaintiff:

Admit or Deny:

> (a) That exhibit "X" attached hereto is a true and correct copy of the assignment of commissions contracts executed by plaintiff on September 10, 1989.

5. Each matter for which an admission is requested shall be deemed admitted unless a written answer or objection is addressed to the matter within 30 days after service of the request.
6. An answering party may not give lack of information or knowledge as a reason for failure to admit or deny unless the party states that the party has made reasonable inquiry and that the information known or readily obtainable is insufficient to enable the party to admit or deny.

Discovery Regarding Expert Witnesses

For federal court cases, Rule 26(b)(4) of the Federal Rules of Civil Procedure specifies the circumstances under which the facts known, and opinions held by expert witnesses, may be obtained in the discovery process. In summary, the federal rules permit the following:

1. A party may submit interrogatories requiring another party to:
   a. Identify each expert witness that party expects to use in the trial of the case.
   b. State the subject matter on which the witness is expected to testify.
   c. State the substance of the facts and opinions to which the expert is expected to testify, and
   d. Present a summary of the grounds for each opinion.
2. A party may discover facts known or opinions held by non-testifying experts retained by an opposing party upon showing of good cause.
3. A party may obtain such appropriate additional discovery of testifying experts as is approved by the court. This will usually be accomplished by deposing the expert witness.
4. The federal rule requires a party to pay part, if not all, of the expenses of an expert witness the party wishes to obtain discovery from.

Although the state rules relative to discovery of expert witnesses are generally similar to the preceding federal rule, there can be some significant variations.

THE TRIAL PROCEEDINGS

At some point, the discovery will be completed, the designated trial date will arrive, and it will be time for the trial proceedings to commence. At this juncture, unless the case is settled or postponed (either of which is entirely possible), the courtroom drama begins—the culmination of many hours of investigation, research, trial discovery, and strategizing. This is also when the expert witness will be called on to "show his [her] stuff" to a live audience—the judge and jury. The trial proceedings consist of a series of steps and procedures leading to the jurors' ultimate decision on the case. Each step plays its vital part in developing the scenario of the case in controversy.

Jury Selection

Once the case is called before the court for trial, the first order of business to be resolved is the picking of a jury. Whether the case involves a civil or a criminal matter, the impaneling of a "fair and impartial" jury is vital to the success of the jury trial process.

The voir dire examination accomplishes this process. The term *voir dire* translates from the French: "to speak the truth." In some jurisdictions, the voir dire examination is conducted primarily by the judge with only limited participation by the trial lawyers; whereas in others the entire process is conducted by the lawyers. This process of questioning the jurors about their background, prejudices, knowledge of the case circumstances, and other related matters enables the lawyers to size up the jurors in their endeavor to seat a "fair and impartial" jury to decide the case. If the questioning process did not take place, the lawyers would not be selecting a jury as such. A panel of jurors would be assigned to the case and that would be that. Unfortunately, such a simplified approach leaves too much room for unfairness or foul play. Most lawyers consider the voir dire to be a crucial part of the litigation proceeding since it provides an opportunity to mold or shape the jury of peers from the panel and to establish rapport and favorable perceptions with the jury selected.

Since the jury is selected before the presentation of any evidence, expert witnesses are not customarily present for this part of the trial proceedings. Nevertheless, it is helpful to know something about this process and how it reflects on the trial proceedings.

After a jury is selected and impaneled, the jurors will be given certain charges and instructions by the judge. Amongst these instructions will be a caveat against discussing the case with anyone else, including each other, the parties, and the witnesses in the case. It is vital that all witnesses be aware of this restriction. Frequently, expert witnesses must kill time outside the courtroom before they are called in to testify and may have occasion to be in the hallway, restrooms, or other common areas with jurors in the case. In such circumstances, the expert should restrict communications to a brief "Hello" or "Good Morning" with a nod or a smile. Anything further may be cause for suspicion and a possible contaminating examination in front of the judge as to what was discussed. In an extreme case, such action could be the basis for being barred from testifying. Obviously, all such complications can be avoided by using discretion and maintaining a proper demeanor. Maintain your distance from jurors until it is your time to be center stage.

Practice Tip: **Also be aware of the presence of jurors when you are conferring with your client or the client's lawyers. Keep your voice in check to avoid being overheard and remember that jurors are watching your actions and body language.**

The Opening Statement

Once the jury is seated, counsel will present their **opening statements**. The plaintiff or prosecutor goes first since they have the **burden of proof**. Lawyers disagree on the importance or value of the opening statement. Its ultimate value probably depends on the type of case, the attitude of the lawyer, and to a large extent the voir dire procedure utilized. If the court has limited the lawyer participation in the voir dire process, the opening statement represents the first real opportunity to focus the jury on your client's position. The attorney who is prepared and effective at "painting word pictures" for the jury can score big points here. Surveys and studies have shown that up to 65 percent of jurors decide the case consistent with their impressions immediately following the opening statements.

An opening statement is like the prologue of a book or a movie preview in that it provides some indication of what is to come. It helps orient the jury and, as previously stated, gives the attorney a chance to focus the minds and impressions of the jurors on factors favorable to his/her client.

The opening statements will generally be disposed of in an hour or less, thus setting the stage for the presentation of the evidence.

Presentation of Evidence

Following the jury selection and opening statements, the attorneys proceed to present the evidence in the case. However, immediately preceding the presentation of the evidence, it is likely that one of the attorneys, or perhaps the judge, will raise the subject of excluding the presence of witnesses in the courtroom while other witnesses are being examined. The rules of procedure in most jurisdictions allow any party to a lawsuit to "invoke the rule" excluding witnesses from the courtroom. The purpose of the rule is to avoid the opportunity for fraud, collusion, perjury, or other such improper practices. Therefore, when the rule is invoked, none of the other witnesses will be allowed in the courtroom while the evidence is being presented until all witnesses have testified and all counsel consent to the witnesses then being allowed in the courtroom. As a practical matter, most lawyers do not want their witnesses in the courtroom, preferring to present them fresh to the jury, thereby creating interest and curiosity. A witness who has been sitting in the courtroom for several days before testifying has more opportunity to influence a juror's impressions in some way, and perhaps negatively.

The evidence to be presented in the case will consist of the testimony of the witnesses, including the expert witness (if any), and the documentary evidence manifested by books, records, files, photos, and other such items. The testimony may be live from the witness stand or may be by deposition testimony. Admissibility, whether by testimony or exhibits, depends on three criteria:

1. Is it **material evidence**?
2. Is it **relevant evidence**?
3. Is it **competent evidence**?

The determination of these three elements is the basis for the objections, motions, colloquy, and other attendant courtroom maneuvering that takes place during any trial as to the admissibility of evidence.

The "Rules of Procedure" and "Rules of Evidence" of the applicable jurisdiction, as well as the attendant case law of that jurisdiction, will govern in making determinations as to the admissibility of evidence.

While as an expert witness, it is helpful to be aware of the basis for such legal maneuvering, there is little you can do except respond to the questions propounded and be guided by the judge's rulings and instructions. Many times, if you have an understanding of the issues being raised by an objection, it may be possible to respond in a manner that alleviates the objection.

For example, if a witness responds to a question during direct examination as follows:

> The chief engineer told me they had been having problems with that mechanism.

the following objection is likely to be quickly voiced:

> Objection—that's hearsay!

However, if the response to the same question was:

> I spent several days studying the situation there at the plant and it appears that there had been several problems in the past with that mechanism.

the response would be less likely to draw an objection even though the same point is made.

For the most part, the raising of objections will depend on the experience of the lawyer and the importance of the admissibility of the discovery tendered.

Jury Argument

Once the evidence has been closed, the case is ready for presentation to the jury. This process is commenced by the closing arguments of counsel to the jury. Generally, each side will have approximately 30 minutes to argue their version of the facts presented by the evidence and how it affects the issues to be decided. In civil cases, the jury may be required to answer a large number of issues although this varies by jurisdiction. In criminal cases the guilt or innocence of the defendant is the issue. Sentencing may be decided at the same time or at a later date, by a judge or by the jury, depending on the case and jurisdiction.

The closing argument also provides attorneys with the opportunity to argue how the law, whether it be **common law**, **case law**, or **statutory law**, affects the case. Presumably, testimony and evidence presented by the expert witnesses will be part of the key evidence argued to the jury. The lawyers may refer to admitted exhibits to advocate their position and are usually permitted to write on charts or a blackboard to visually emphasize their points.

After the attorneys have concluded their jury argument, the jurors will retire to the jury room to make their decisions in accordance with the court's charge. Exhibit 1-1 shows a typical court's charge in a civil matter and illustrates the sort of instructions given to the jurors by the judge. Attached to the court's charge will be the special issues to be answered by the jurors in the case. The number and broadness of other issues may vary by jurisdiction, as well as the type of case involved.

In addition, if the court decides that any definitions or instructions are required to clarify the issues in the case for jurors,

EXHIBIT 1-1

CHARGE OF THE COURT

MEMBERS OF THE JURY:

This case is submitted to you on special issues consisting of specific questions about the facts, which you must decide from the evidence you have heard in this trial. You are the sole judges of the credibility of the witnesses and the weight to be given their testimony; but in matters of law, you must be governed by the instructions in this charge. In discharging your responsibility on this jury, you will observe all the instructions that have previously been given you. I shall now give you additional instructions that you should carefully and strictly follow during your deliberations.

1. Do not let bias, prejudice, or sympathy play any part in your deliberations.
2. In arriving at your answers, consider only the evidence introduced here under oath and such exhibits, if any, as have been introduced for your consideration under the rulings of the Court; that is, what you have seen and heard in this courtroom, together with the law as given you by the Court. In your deliberations, you will not consider or discuss anything that is not represented by the evidence in this case.
3. Since every answer that is required by the charge is important, no juror should state or consider that any required answer is not important.
4. You must not decide who you think should win, and then try to answer the questions accordingly. Simply answer the questions, and do not discuss nor concern yourselves with the effect of your answers.
5. You may render your verdict upon the vote of five or more members of the jury. The same five or more of you must agree upon all of the answers made, and to the entire verdict. You will not, therefore, enter into an agreement to be bound by a majority or any other vote of less than five jurors. If the verdict and all of the answers therein are reached by unanimous agreement, the presiding juror shall sign the verdict for the entire jury. If any juror disagrees as to any answer made by the verdict, those jurors who agree to all findings shall each sign the verdict.

EXHIBIT 1-1 *(continued)*

These instructions are given you because your conduct is subject to review the same as that of the witnesses, parties, attorneys and the judge. If it should be found that you have disregarded any of these instructions, it will be jury misconduct and it may require another trial by another jury; then all our time will have been wasted.

The presiding juror or any other juror who observes a violation of the Court's instructions shall immediately warn the one who is violating the same and caution the juror not to do so again.

When words are used in special issues in a sense that varies from the meaning commonly understood, you will be given in this charge a proper legal definition, which you are bound to accept in place of any other definition or meaning.

Answer "Yes" or "No" unless otherwise instructed. A "Yes" answer must be based on a preponderance of the evidence. If you do not find that a preponderance of the evidence supports a "Yes" answer, then answer "No."

"PREPONDERANCE OF THE EVIDENCE" means the greater weight and degree of credible testimony or evidence introduced before you and admitted in this case.

After you retire to the jury room, you will select your own presiding juror. The first thing the presiding juror will do is to have this complete charge read aloud and then you will deliberate upon your answers to the questions asked.

It is the duty of the presiding juror:

1. To preside during your deliberations.
2. To see that your deliberations are conducted in an orderly manner and in accordance with the instructions in this charge.
3. To write out and hand to the bailiff any communication concerning the case that you desire to have delivered to the judge.
4. To vote on the issues.
5. To write your answers to the issues in the spaces provided.
6. To certify to your verdict in the space provided for the presiding juror's signature or to obtain the signatures of all the jurors who agree with the verdict if your verdict is less than unanimous.

After you have retired to consider your verdict, no one has any authority to communicate with you except the bailiff of this court.

EXHIBIT 1-1 *(continued)*

You should not discuss the case with anyone, not even with other members of the jury, unless all of you are present and assembled in the jury room. Should anyone attempt to talk to you about the case before the verdict is returned, whether at the courthouse, at your home, or elsewhere, please inform the judge of this fact.

When you have answered all the questions that you are required to answer under the instructions of the Judge, and your presiding juror has placed your answers in the spaces provided and signed the verdict as presiding juror or obtained the signatures, you will advise the bailiff at the door of the jury room that you have reached a verdict, and then you will return into court with your verdict.

____

Judge
Court No. 1

CERTIFICATE

We, the Jury, have answered the above and foregoing questions as herein indicated and herewith return same into court as our verdict.

(To be signed by the presiding juror if unanimous)

____

PRESIDING JUROR

(To be signed by those rendering the verdict if not unanimous)

____

____

____

____

____

they will be included with the court's charge and attached special issues.

The **court's charge**, definitions, and instructions and special issues, constitute the complete package presented to jurors to serve as their road map for deliberations in the case. In addition, they will be entitled to receive all the exhibits admitted into evidence in the case for review and examination.

The pleadings form the basis of the issues in the case, the evidence delineates the issues, and the court's charge and special issues puts all the factors of the case into perspective for decision by the jurors.

Post-Trial Procedures

Once the jury has deliberated and rendered its decisions, the judge will release them from the case. However, many other procedures may be involved before the case is actually finalized.

The first concern will be the **entry of judgment** in the case. This may be a straightforward procedure or may involve motions for a new trial, new **indictment**, **Judgment N.O.V.**, or other matters. Even after a judgment is entered, the case may be appealed. Since the appellate process does not generally involve the expert witness, no effort is made to detail that process in this book. The most salient feature of the appellate process is the related delay and expense and the effect of this delay on the ultimate results in the case.

KEY WORDS AND PHRASES

Note: Many of the definitions in this book are extracted entirely or in part from *Black's Law Dictionary, Sixth Edition,* copyright © 1990 by West Publishing Co., St. Paul, Minnesota, and are reprinted with permission.

Admissible evidence Evidence of such a character that the court or judge is bound to receive it; that is, allow it to be introduced.

Appellate jurisdiction The power and authority to take cognizance of a cause and proceed to its determination after it has been finally decided by an inferior court. Involves the power to correct errors in judgment under review or to make such disposition of causes as justice may require.

Burden of proof The necessity or duty of affirmatively proving a fact or facts in dispute on an issue raised between the parties in a cause.

Case law The body of law based on case decisions as precedent in distinction to statutes and other sources of law.

Civil action An adversary proceeding for declaration, enforcement, or protection of a right, or redress or prevention of a wrong. Every action other than a criminal action.

Common law Distinguishable from legislative law and comprising the principles and rules of action that derive their authority from usage and custom.

Competent evidence Evidence that is generally admissible or relevant.

Concurrent jurisdiction The jurisdiction of several different tribunals, each authorized to deal with the same subject-matter at the choice of the *suitor.*

Court's charge The instructions by the judge to the jury designed to guide them in their case determination.

Deposition The out-of-court process of obtaining oral statements of a party or witness under oath and recording them in written form. Intended for use in the trial of an action in court.

Discovery The process of securing knowledge and evidence in the opposing party's possession.

Entry of judgment The formal entry of the judgment on the roles of the court, which is necessary before bringing an appeal or an action on the judgment. It differs from "rendition of judgment," which is the judicial act of the judge in pronouncing the sentence or decision of the law on the facts in controversy. The "entry" is a ministerial act.

Evidence Any species of proof, or probative matter, legally presented at the trial of an issue through the medium of witnesses, records, documents, concrete objects, and so on for the purpose of inducing belief in the minds of the court or jury as to their contentions.

Expert witness One who has skilled experience or extensive knowledge in his/her calling or any branch of learning. Persons selected by the court, or parties in a cause, on account of their knowledge or skill, to examine, estimate, and ascertain things and make a report of their opinions.

Indictment An accusation in writing found and presented by a grand jury charging that a person has done some act or is guilty of a public offense.

Interrogatories A set or series of written questions drawn up for the purpose of being propounded by one party to another requiring written answers under oath.

Judgment N.O.V. (Non Obstante Veredicto) A judgment entered by the court for one party, although a verdict has been found for the other party.

Jurisdiction The authority, capacity, power, or right of a court to act (may also be used to mean only venue).

Lay witness A nonprofessional witness.

Magistrate Generally refers to a lower level judicial officer such as a justice of the peace.

Materiality of evidence "Materiality" of evidence refers to pertinency of the offered evidence to the issue in dispute.

Opening statement of counsel An address to the jury designed to give a general picture of the facts and the situations so that the jury will be able to understand the evidence.

Plaintiff The party who complains or sues in a personal action and is so named on the record.

Pleading The formal allegations by the parties to a lawsuit of their respective claims and defenses with the intended purpose being to provide notice of what is to be expected at trial.

Relevant evidence Evidence tending to prove or disprove an alleged fact.

Request for admissions A legal discovery document requiring the opposing party either to admit or deny certain statements of fact or law propounded to them for response in writing and under oath.

Special issues In some jurisdictions, the specific questions to be answered by the jury in case deliberation.

Special master Magistrate having authority to act as the court's representative in particular or specialized acts or transactions.

Statutory law The body of law based on legislative or congressional enactments.

Venue The geographical division in which an action or prosecution is brought for trial.

Voir dire Literally, "To speak the truth." This phrase denotes the preliminary examination that the court may make of an individual presented as a witness or juror.

CHAPTER 2

The Role of the Expert Witness

In today's legal environment, a trial frequently becomes a battle of experts. Often the case turns into a tug-of-war between the plaintiff's experts and the defendant's experts. This scenario has created an increasing demand for experts, especially in product liability cases, professional malpractice matters, and other cases involving complex technical issues and substantial damages.

I recently read the following passage in "Coppalino Revisited," by John D. McDonald (*Solved and Unsolved Classic True Murder Cases,* New York: Bonanza Books) about the 1967 trial of Carl Coppalino, anesthesiologist, who was convicted of second-degree murder for killing his wife with an injection of succinylcholine chloride, a paralyzing compound used to stop the patient from breathing on his own during major surgery on the lungs or heart. In the conduct of his defense, F. Lee Bailey barraged the jury with a team of experts calculated to refute the condemning medical testimony presented by the prosecution.

> What do we have then, in this and in other trials where contemporary expert testimony is given by both sides? Not one of

> those twelve jurors knew diddly about anesthesiology, toxicology, biochemistry, and pharmacology. They could not follow and comprehend the expert testimony. The prosecution lawyers and the defense lawyers knew that the jurors could not follow the expert testimony and evaluate it upon its scientific merits. The experts knew this also.
>
> So it is a charade.
>
> Recognizing the fact of charade, one realizes that the jurors will side with that expert who has the best stage presence, who radiates a total confidence in his grasp of the subject at hand, who speaks crisply, with dignity, confidence, and charm, who is neatly and properly dressed and has no distressing mannerisms.
>
> In short, the expert must be precisely the sort of person an advertising agency would select to talk about a new deodorant on national television.
>
> The expert who mumbles, slouches, grimaces, stares into space, and keeps ramming his little finger into his ear and inspecting what he dredges up might be a far better scientist than the television commercial chap. But there is no real correlation here. The impressive presence is more likely to be the result of the number of appearances as an expert than the result of academic credentials.
>
> The question is obvious. How can jurors make honest judgments about a body of knowledge beyond their capacity to comprehend?

Although the foregoing quote expresses some despair with the system, it likewise depicts the nature of the beast and how integrally involved the expert witness has become with the litigation process as we know it today.

While the qualified and seasoned expert may be able to radiate the persona, charm, and confidence chided by McDonald, many novice or would-be expert witnesses feel less comfortable with their role. No doubt sitting on the witness stand to give expert testimony as well as confront cross-examination is a rigorous challenge. To some, it may resemble being staked out on an anthill in the hot desert sun while coated with honey. To others, it's akin to wrestling with a rattlesnake: "It's a great sport if you don't get bit."

Trial lawyers receive extensive information and training on how to deal with expert witnesses—how to cross-examine, how to prepare, and how to hire such witnesses. The problem is that most expert witnesses do not receive equal training and preparation. While a plethora of literature is available to lawyers on this subject, relatively few guidebooks or articles have been written for the expert witness.

Nonetheless, there is no need to despair. Experience is a great teacher, and with proper training and guidance, you can "hold your own." This book is filled with information and tips that will help you do just that. The downside of courtroom confrontation may be that you are walking on the other party's turf, but the upside is that the questioning and examination are on *your* subject, an area with which you are uniquely acquainted and possess exceptional knowledge and expertise.

> ***Practice Tip:*** **Sometimes the case in which you are involved may be the lawyers' first exposure to such subject matter. The lawyers' knowledge of the subject may be limited to what they have learned secondhand from their expert in the case. Be alert for the opposing lawyer who does not appear to be well-versed about relevant technical information because that is your opportunity to score points for your client.**

WHO QUALIFIES AS AN EXPERT WITNESS

Black's Law Dictionary defines an expert witness as follows:

> One who by reason of education or experience possesses superior knowledge respecting a subject about which persons having no particular training are incapable of forming an accurate opinion or deducing correct conclusions. A witness who has been qualified

as an expert and who thereby will be allowed (through his/her answers to questions posted) to assist the jury in understanding complicated and technical subjects not within the understanding of the average lay person. One possessing, with reference to a particular subject, knowledge not acquired by ordinary persons. One skilled in any particular art, trade, or profession, being possessed of peculiar knowledge concerning the same, and one who has given the subject in question particular study, practice, or observation. One who by habits of life and business has peculiar skill in forming opinion on subject in dispute.

Black's also defines the concept of expert testimony:

Opinion evidence of some person who possesses special skill or knowledge in some science, profession or business which is not common to the average man and which is possessed by the expert by reason of his special study or experience. Testimony given in relation to some scientific, technical, or professional matter by experts, i.e. persons qualified to speak authoritatively by reason of their special training, skill, or familiarity with the subject. Evidence of persons who are skilled in some art, science, profession, or business, which skill or knowledge is not common to their fellow men, and which has come to such experts by reason of special study and experience in such art, science, profession, or business.

If scientific, technology, or other specialized knowledge will assist the trier of fact to understand the evidence or to determine a fact in issue, a witness qualified as an expert by knowledge, skill experience, training, or education, may testify thereto in the form of an opinion or otherwise. Fed. Evid.R. 702, 703.

Practice Tip: **If you don't already have a *Black's Law Dictionary* (West Publishing Company, St. Paul, Minnesota), I strongly recommend that you acquire one. It contains all you ever wanted to know about legal terms and phrases.**

The foregoing definitions clearly express the role and purpose of the expert witness. Nevertheless, the courts often struggle with whether a proposed witness qualifies as an expert witness pursuant to the applicable Rules of Evidence and Procedure. It is virtually impossible to establish a specific set of guidelines for determining the knowledge, experience, or skill required to qualify automatically as an expert witness.

Trial judges generally possess broad discretion in making their determination as to the admissibility of expert testimony. In making its determination, the court may, and does, analyze the basis of the expert's opinions and personal knowledge of the facts to determine whether such testimony will aid the jury in resolving the issues involved in the case.

An individual can qualify as an expert on the basis of experience or training; a formal education is not a prerequisite. The burden of establishing the expert's qualifications falls on the party offering the testimony. As an expert witness, you should not agree to testify in areas beyond your scope of expertise since the inability to establish qualifications on the subject may cast a shadow on your credibility.

The Federal Jury Instruction Guide tells the jury:

> If you should decide that the opinion of an expert witness is not based upon sufficient education and experience, or if you should conclude that the reasons given in support of the opinion are not sound, or that the opinion is outweighed by other evidence, you may disregard the opinion entirely.

Various court opinions have established factors that may be considered in determining whether a proposed expert is qualified to testify. The following is a partial nonexclusive list of factors extracted from various case opinions:

1. Extent of education and training.
2. Amount of experience.

3. Membership on committees and professional organizations.
4. Speeches given on the subject.
5. Participation in studies or research relating to the field.
6. Publication of books, articles, or professional papers.
7. Involvement in surveys on the topic.
8. Degree of present involvement in the field or profession (i.e., is a substantial part of the individual's time devoted to active involvement in the field or profession).
9. Teaching of the subject matter.
10. Reliability of the underlying data on which the expert's opinion is based (general scientific recognition).
11. Established familiarity with the precise subject matter involved.
12. Degree of personal knowledge of pertinent facts in the case.

While these factors enable the court to evaluate the qualifications of the proposed expert and the competency of the testimony, the bottom line is whether the testimony will assist the jury in making a proper decision.

Even after the court determines that the expert is properly qualified and allows the testimony, the jury may also consider the foregoing factors in determining the degree of credibility and believability to assign the testimony.

HOW THE RULES OF EVIDENCE AFFECT THE EXPERT'S TESTIMONY

The applicable rules of evidence provide ample guidance relative to witnesses and expert testimony. The following discussion is based on the Federal Rules of Evidence. Many states base their Rules of Evidence on the Federal Rules while others deviate in varying degrees.

- *General Rule of Competency (Rule 601).* Every person is deemed to be competent to be a witness except as otherwise specified in the Federal Rules. However, as to civil cases and criminal cases involving state law, the law of the applicable state governs competency.
- *Lack of Personal Knowledge (Rule 602).* This rule states that witnesses may not testify to a matter unless sufficient evidence is introduced to support a finding that the witness has personal knowledge of the matter. Personal knowledge, however, is not required of the expert witness (per Rule 703).
- *Who May Impeach (Rule 607).* This rule, which relates to **impeachment of witnesses**, allows lawyers to attack the credibility of any witness, including their own.
- *Evidence of Character and Conduct of Witnesses (Rule 608).* Rule 608 permits attacks on the credibility of a witness by establishing a reputation for lack of truthfulness.
- *Impeachment by Evidence of Conviction of Crime (Rule 609).* Under Rule 609, evidence is permitted that a witness has been convicted of any crime involving dishonesty or a false statement or any crime punishable by death or more than one-year imprisonment, providing the court determines that the probative value of such evidence outweighs the prejudicial affect to the accused. However, evidence of convictions more than 10 years old are not permitted, unless the court determines that the **probative value** of the conviction substantially outweighs its prejudicial effect. Notice must be given to the **adverse party** of the intent to use such evidence, sufficient to provide the adverse party with a fair opportunity to contest its use. The right to use such evidence may be limited or disallowed in the event of pardon, annulment, or certificate of rehabilitation.

  The pendency of an appeal does not render evidence of a conviction inadmissible.

- *Religious Beliefs or Opinions (Rule 610).* Evidence of the beliefs or opinions of a witness on matters of religion is not admissible for the purpose of showing that by reason of their nature, the credibility of the witness is either impaired or enhanced.
- *Mode and Order of Interrogation and Presentation (Rule 611).* Rule 611 grants the court reasonable control over the mode and order of interrogating witnesses and presenting evidence. Generally, **cross-examination** is limited to matters within the scope of the **direct examination** unless the court exercises discretion to permit inquiry into additional matters as if on direct examination.

  Leading questions are ordinarily permitted in cross-examination or on direct examination of adverse parties or witnesses identified with the adverse party.

  The overall objective is to avoid wasting time, effectuate the ascertainment of truth, and protect witnesses from harassment or undue embarrassment.
- *Writing Used to Refresh Memory (Rule 612).* The important point here is that if a witness uses a writing to refresh memory for purposes of testifying, an adverse party is entitled to inspect the writing and cross-examine the witness thereon. Those portions of the document relating to the testimony of the witness may be introduced into evidence. This rule pertains to *any* writing and therefore includes any notes made by the expert in preparing to give testimony. This rule may even apply before the witness testifies as well as during the witness's testimony.

Practice Tip: **Make sure the lawyer for your client is fully aware of any notes or writings in your possession to avoid any embarrassment or potentially damaging events.**

- *Prior Statements of Witnesses (Rule 613).* This rule provides guidelines as to the examination of witnesses relative to prior statements made by them that may be inconsistent with their testimony in the actual trial on the case. If this occurs, a lawyer has the right to request disclosure of the contents of such a statement. Generally an opportunity will also be provided to explain or deny the statement.
- *Opinion Testimony by Lay Witnesses (Rule 701).* This rule and Rule 602 both apply to witnesses who are not testifying as experts. Rule 701 limits the witness's opinions or inferences to those that are rationally based on the perception of the witness and that are helpful to a clear understanding of the testimony or the determination of a fact issue.

The combined effect of Rules 602 and 701 is to limit the testimony of lay witnesses to matters of personal knowledge or such opinions and inferences derived from the personal knowledge as a normal person would form from such perceptions and knowledge.

In actual practice, applying these Rules can be difficult because the trial court has a great deal of discretion in determining whether any particular lay opinion will be admissible. This has resulted in extensive case law pertaining to the admissibility of testimony. Case law has generally established that lay witnesses can give opinions on matters such as the following, if they meet the provisos of Rules 602 and 701:

1. The witness's own physical health and condition.
2. That someone is of unsound mind.
3. Handwriting.
4. Estimates of age, size, weight, quantity, time, speed, quality, and other similar matters.
5. Impressions as to another's health and condition.
6. Statements of market value of the witness's own property.
7. Opinions as to the cause of a particular accident or occurrence.

■ *Testimony by Experts (Rule 702)*

If scientific, technical or other specialized knowledge will assist the trier of the fact to understand the evidence or to determine a fact in issue, a witness qualified as an expert by knowledge, skill, experience, training or education, may testify thereto in the form of an opinion or otherwise.

The above verbatim statement of the Rule sets the standard for federal courts and many state courts for the utilization of expert testimony in lawsuits. This rule expands beyond the testimony permitted by lay witnesses under Rules 602 and 701.

Although Rule 702 is relatively brief and concise, there has been longstanding controversy and deliberation over the expanse of the Rules of Evidence relative to the admission of expert testimony. In recent years, the trend has clearly favored the use of expert testimony, and the Rules of Evidence have been liberally construed to accommodate that trend.

An analysis of the application of Rule 702 reflects several areas of inquiry that become relevant in applying the Rule. For example:

1. What type of subject matter qualifies as *specialized knowledge?*
2. Does the witness have the requisite *qualifications* of an expert?
3. What degree of *assistance* or clarification must the expert testimony provide the trier of fact?

In effect, the Rule establishes a three-pronged test for the admissibility of expert testimony:

1. Specialized knowledge.
2. Qualifications.
3. Assistance to jurors.

While these requisite elements are problems for the lawyers and the courts to resolve, a solid understanding of what's involved not only will make you a better prepared witness but also will apprise you of the extent of opportunity available to you as an expert.

Bases of Opinion Testimony by Experts (Rule 703)

The facts or data in the particular case upon which an expert bases an opinion or inference may be those perceived by or made known to the expert at or before the hearing. If of a type reasonably relied upon by experts in the particular field in forming opinions or inferences upon the subject, the facts or data need not be admissible in evidence.

This rule allows experts to base their opinions and testimony on any of the following:

1. Personal knowledge and observations.
2. Admissible facts perceived by or made known to the expert at or before the trial.
3. Inadmissible facts perceived by or made known to the expert at or before the trial, providing it is information reasonably relied on by experts in the field.

Although your testimony must have probative value and reliability to be admissible in the trial of the case, the facts or data on which it is based may be considered by the trier of fact in determining how much weight and credibility to give to your testimony. Obviously testimony based on your personal knowledge or observations will carry the most weight.

The effect of the third part of this three-pronged criterion is to allow expert opinions and testimony based on **hearsay**. However, the extent to which the expert can rely on hearsay evidence may vary by jurisdiction since the courts continue to be protective of the applicable Rules of Evidence regarding hearsay evidence. Accordingly, many courts allow expert testimony that is based in part on hearsay, but some will not allow expert testimony if it is based entirely on hearsay. Further, the value of the hearsay must also be considered. In other words, is the hearsay information of a type that would reasonably be relied on by experts in that particular field? As a general rule, the courts want to avoid the use of experts as a means of avoiding or undermining the hearsay rule, which would otherwise disallow testimony based on statements of others.

Article VIII (Rules 801–805) of the Federal Rules of Evidence provides extensive guidance on the Hearsay Rule and its application. Rule 801 defines hearsay, and Rule 802 states that hearsay is not admissible except as otherwise provided by the rules.

> ***Practice Tip:*** **The relevant test on hearsay matters is not what the court considers reliable but what experts in the relevant discipline consider it to be. Refer to Chapter 8 for further discussion of the hearsay rules.**

- *Opinion on Ultimate Issue (Rule 704).* The effect of Rule 704 is to allow any witness to give testimony in the form of opinions or inferences on the **ultimate issues** in the case as long as such testimony would otherwise be admissible. This broad rule, however, does not apply to expert witnesses with respect to the mental state or condition of a defendant in a criminal case constituting an element of the crime or a defense thereto. For example, under this rule, an expert witness in a product liability case would be allowed to testify that a particular design was unreasonably dangerous. However, to the extent that testimony of this type delves into questions of law rather than questions of fact, it is likely that such evidence would not be admissible in many jurisdictions.

  Typically such matters are essentially the province of the judge and the lawyers. Nonetheless, an expert who has a good basic grasp of the procedural and evidentiary rules is better prepared to deal with the process.

> ***Practice Tip:*** **An important part of thorough preparation is learning what you can and cannot properly testify to. Do not hesitate to discuss these issues with your client's lawyer so you will know how to proceed.**

■ *Disclosure of Facts or Data Underlying Expert Opinion (Rule 705).*

> The expert may testify in terms of opinion or inference and give reasons therefore without prior disclosure of the underlying facts or data, unless the court requires otherwise. The expert may in any event be required to disclose the underlying facts or data on cross-examination.

Like many of the current Rules of Evidence, this rule is much broader and more liberal than was the case a decade or so ago.

The current Rules of Evidence in most jurisdictions favor liberal admissibility of evidence; deeming it to be faster, fairer, and more efficient. This type of rule streamlines the lawyers' presentation of evidence. It eliminates the requirement of asking hypothetical questions involving a summary of the facts and details of the case. It also permits the lawyer to ask for your opinions on key issues at the inception of your testimony while the jury is curious and attentive. The underlying facts or data, which are often tedious and lengthy, can be included later in the direct examination or left to cross-examination.

The effect of the broad implementation of Rule 705 in most jurisdictions puts more pressure on the cross-examiner to probe the bases of your opinion. It also leaves the cross-examiner open to ambush if you have not been thoroughly deposed on these matters prior to trial. As a result, expert witnesses are almost always deposed prior to trial.

Although no longer required, many lawyers still prefer to use **hypothetical questions** since they give the lawyer an extra opportunity to focus the jury on key points of evidence by summarizing those points in the questions.

> ***Practice Tip:***
>
> 1. **The lawyer is not required to put all the facts into a hypothetical question (i.e., those facts that are contrary to your client's position in the case). So be prepared to deal with those matters on cross-examination.**
> 2. **Be certain that your client's lawyer prepares you in detail on any hypothetical questions that will be asked at trial, including hypotheticals based on the cross-examiner's version of the facts and theory of the case.**

- *Court-Appointed Experts (Rule 706).* In addition to expert witnesses designated by the parties in the case, Rule 706 enables the court to appoint expert witnesses on its own motion or the motion of any party. The experts appointed may be by agreement of the parties or of the court's own selection. The court will inform such witnesses in writing of the duties to be performed. Court-appointed experts are required to report their findings in the case to all parties. Any party may depose a court-appointed expert witness and is entitled to cross-examine the witness in the trial of the case if the expert is called to testify.

  The court has full authority and discretion to establish the reasonable compensation to be paid to appointed experts.

  The court also has discretion to inform the jury that the court appointed the expert witness. On occasion, this may be impressive to the jury since it signifies that the expert is independent of the parties in the case. Thus, Rule 706 provides an additional opportunity for employment for the expert witness.

SCOPE OF THE EXPERT'S ENGAGEMENT

Experts may be hired for a number of different reasons including the following primary categories:

1. Investigative Experts.
2. Consulting Experts.
3. Testifying Experts.

In most jurisdictions, the status of the expert may have some bearing on the discoverability of the expert's data.

Investigative Experts

These experts are retained by the client or their counsel to perform specific duties such as test a product, analyze an accident scene, inspect property damage, locate and interview witnesses, or other such matters. The facts of the case will govern the degree of this expert's involvement. Generally, their purpose will be to perform limited preparatory functions. Often such experts are hired strictly to provide information that will enable the attorney to better evaluate the case. In such instances, the expert may never be identified as an expert depending on the law in the applicable jurisdiction. In other jurisdictions, the investigative witness may be considered to be the same as a consulting expert.

Consulting Experts

A consulting expert is engaged solely for the purpose of providing advice, preparation, and assistance in a legal matter. Of course, it is possible that the consulting expert may later be asked to serve as a testifying expert as well. The law of some jurisdictions, Texas, for example, is such that the mental impressions, opinions, reports, or identity of a consulting expert are not discoverable unless such information forms the basis of an opinion of a testifying expert. In such situations, it is very important that the status of the expert be properly classified for purpose of trial tactics and discovery.

The work to be performed by the consulting expert will generally be directed by the client's attorney and may be broad or specific in scope depending on the circumstances. For example, a retired insurance adjuster might be hired to help explain the provisions of an insurance policy and the inner workings of the insurance claims department to the plaintiff's lawyer without any intent of calling that person as a witness. In this case, the consulting expert could perform a variety of functions including attendance at meetings with opposing insurance personnel, mapping of strategy, and organizing the insurance materials for quick review and reference.

Testifying Experts

The rules of procedure in most jurisdictions require the parties to designate their testifying experts as part of the discovery in the case. They may also be required to disclose the subject matter on which the witness is expected to testify, the mental impressions and opinions held by the expert, and the facts known to the expert that relate to or form the basis of the mental impressions and opinions held by the expert. Generally, this information must be disclosed at least 30 days prior to the trial of the case and perhaps longer depending on the jurisdiction.

Therefore, as a potential expert, you will want to know in what status you are being engaged, not only so you can be informed as to your commitment but also so you will know how you should prepare yourself. Your client's attorney can apprise you how the law operates in his/her jurisdiction and whether certain things should be done. For example, the lawyer may prefer that you do not prepare any written reports since they could be used to prepare for your cross-examination and pose possible impeachment traps.

> ***Practice Tip:*** **Always inquire as to the applicable law of the jurisdiction so you don't do anything that could possibly cause problems or embarrassment for you or your client.**

CRITERIA USED BY ATTORNEYS IN SELECTING EXPERTS

In most instances, the client's attorney will be the one who contacts you about serving as an expert witness. Unless the attorney is already acquainted with you and your abilities, he or she will most likely want to screen you in many particulars prior to offering engagement. Generally, by the time you are contacted, the client's attorney will have carefully analyzed the case and will know the points in the case that need to be established by the testimony. As previously discussed, attorneys sometimes seek consulting assistance only. If this is the case, your reputation and knowledge will be the primary criteria under consideration. If the attorney is seeking a testifying expert, however, the selection criteria will be considerably more comprehensive. The following factors are frequently considered by attorneys in selecting a testifying expert.

- *Education.* What is your educational background? Is it strong in the precise field under scrutiny? How current is your continuing education in the field? How well do you detail your educational background when asked? Did you attend recognized schools? How was your class standing? Did you receive any academic honors? What degrees do you have?

In short, the attorney is seeking an expert witness whose education not only extends beyond that of the average juror but also stands out in the field and causes colleagues to recognize the witness with respect.

- *Experience.* Education without experience is not a sound basis for expert testimony. On the other hand, good solid practical experience combined with the respect of your professional peers can be the foundation for very effective expert testimony. Jurors tend to lend credibility to the witness who has substantial "hands on" experience providing the testimony is presented knowledgeably and convincingly.
- *Appearance and Demeanor.* These factor plays a big part in the selection of a testifying expert. The appearance and outward behavior of a witness significantly influence the perceptions of jurors. How you sit, how you dress, the sound of your voice, your grooming, and your general presence are all important. Do you seem pompous or "stuffy"? Do you give the appearance of being candid and impartial or sly and secretive?

  Some things we cannot change about ourselves. If, for example, you are 70 years old, you are not going to look 30 years old and vice versa. But we do have control over most aspects of appearance. Do what is necessary to present yourself in the best possible light.

Practice Tip: **The attorney will be sizing you up based on the impression you would likely make on the jury. If you don't make a good impression with the attorney, don't expect to get hired.**

- *Ability to Communicate.* This is another crucial factor. The whole purpose of an expert witness at the trial is to break down complicated facts so that the jury can understand them. Regardless of your educational background and experience, if you cannot explain your subject matter and opinions so that a jury can understand and relate to them, you will not be a successful expert witness. If you cannot make the jury understand, you have not accomplished your mission no matter how intelligent or valid your opinions may be.

In addition, it is necessary to make your presentation in a relaxed and confident manner so you do not alienate or offend the jury.

> ***Practice Tip:*** **Practice your delivery before a mirror and record your voice for review and improvement. If you think you need further improvement or polishing, consider joining a Toastmasters group or obtain private tutoring.**

- *Price.* As is usually the case, price is a factor although it is not necessarily a primary factor. Frequently, the client's budget or ability to pay will play a part in how much expense can be allocated for expert witness testimony.

  Most trial attorneys have a working knowledge of what constitutes reasonable rates for expert testimony. If your fees appear out of line, it will impair your chances of being hired. See Chapter 3 for a more detailed discussion on fee setting.
- *Availability.* Many times, attorneys are down to the deadline when they are looking for an expert. This is important because the attorney who fails to name an expert by the cutoff date may waive the right to use an expert at trial. Although this dilemma may cause the attorney to be less picky in making the selection, the availability of the witness to act immediately becomes essential. The attorney may need to have you available for immediate deposition preparation and will want to assure your availability for any scheduled trial setting.

Your geographical accessibility may also be important. For example, are you in a location that makes it feasible for you to appear at the designated courthouse or the attorney's office within a reasonable time?

Although the foregoing factors are not all-encompassing, they do reflect the attorney's primary considerations in choosing expert witnesses.

THE PRE-ENGAGEMENT INTERVIEW

The preceding factors are evaluated during the pre-engagement interview.

Although in some cases you may be engaged based on a telephone conversation, at other times a personal interview may be necessary. In either instance, the attorney and the expert need to discuss a number of facts and make decisions pursuant to finalizing the engagement.

You should be prepared to discuss the following inquiries initially:

- *General Information.* In every instance, you must be prepared to discuss your fees, availability, expenses, and similar matters.
- *Conflicts of Interest.* An immediate determination must be made as to whether you have any familiarity with the case or any conflicts evolving from prior or present dealings with any of the parties or attorneys involved. Have you testified previously on a similar case? Have you had problems with any of the other lawyers in the case? These types of inquiries enable the lawyer to determine if the proposed expert is carrying any "excess baggage." These issues should be addressed and discussed thoroughly at the outset of the case before the lawyer designates you as an expert. Lawyers don't like surprises, and clients do not like to pay for useless services. For

example, if an undisclosed conflict develops, the lawyer may decide that they cannot continue with your services and the client will have to incur additional costs in starting all over with a different expert. In some cases, it may even be too late to do so.

- *Initial Reaction.* The lawyer will be interested in your initial reaction to the case. How does it sound to you? Make certain the facts are reasonably clear before you tender your impressions. Obviously, you are limited at this juncture in expressing an opinion until you have studied the facts. The main consideration is that there is no point in involving you in the case if you are not comfortable with the facts or nature of the case. What is your "gut reaction"?
- *Expertise.* Do you have expertise on the precise subject matter involved? Are you the best person for the job, or would another field of expertise be more applicable? You cannot be all things to all people. Although it may be your field, does it involve an aspect somewhat remote to you? Be honest with yourself and be honest with the inquirer. Your reputation is on the line and if you put the client in jeopardy by being greedy for business it will come back to haunt you.
- *Court Room Experience.* The lawyer will want to know how many cases you have testified in and what deposition experience you have had. What courts? What type of cases? Where? Have you ever testified in their jurisdiction?

  Negative answers will not necessarily be held against you. The questions are simply part of the overall evaluation process.
- *Past History.* The inquirer may seek information as to the subject matter of cases you have worked on and the nature of your opinions. They will also be interested in what side of the docket you have worked on. Do you have experience on both sides of the docket so as to give an appearance of being totally objective rather than being a "hired gun"?

- *Advertising.* Have you advertised for business in the past? If so, the lawyer may want to review your past claims and assertions to consider how they may be used against you by an effective cross-examiner.
- *Publications.* The lawyer may wish to review any articles, books, or papers you have written to determine whether there are inconsistencies relative to the issues of their case. Past writings can also be an effective tool for the cross-examiner. Be prepared to discuss these matters in the engagement process.
- *References.* The lawyer may be interested in a list of the lawyers' names in other cases where you have testified in order to discuss your performance with them or possibly obtain copies of depositions or transcripts of trial testimony for review.
- *Engagement.* Be wary of a tentative arrangement unless you have received a reasonable retainer. Once you commit or receive any meaningful information, you will not be able to work for anyone else in the case. Many lawyers like to get the key experts tied up so the other side can't use them. That may be acceptable if you receive a fee, but you will be unhappy if you don't receive any payment for your tentative engagement and have to turn down other paying offers. The following chapter contains additional information and practice pointers regarding the engagement process.

KEY WORDS AND PHRASES

Adverse party Synonymous with opposing party.

Cross-examination The examination of a witness at a trial or hearing, or upon taking a deposition, by the party opposed to the party who called that witness, to test the truth or further develop it.

Direct examination The first interrogation or examination of a witness, on the merits, by the party on whose behalf he is called.

Hearsay Testimony given by a witness who relates not what he knows personally, but what others have told him or what he has heard said by others.

Hypothetical question A hypothetical question is a form of question framed in such a manner as to call for an opinion from an expert based on a series of assumptions claimed to have been established as fact by the evidence in a case. It is a device which is used at trial to enable an expert witness to express an opinion concerning facts about which he did not have personal knowledge. It should be so framed as to recite all the facts in evidence which are relevant to the formation of an opinion and then, assuming the facts recited to be true, the witness should be asked whether he is able to form an opinion therefrom and if so to state his opinion.

Impeachment of witness To call in question the veracity of a witness, by means of evidence adduced for such purpose, or the adducing of proof that a witness is unworthy of belief.

Probative value Evidence has "probative value" if it tends to prove an issue.

Ultimate issue That question which must finally be answered as, for example, the defendants negligence is the ultimate issue in a personal injury action.

CHAPTER 3

Marketing and Getting Hired

Although abundant opportunities exist for expert witnesses, the competition can be fierce. It is not enough simply to pronounce, "I are one." First, you must establish yourself as a successful consultant, and second, you must make your availability known. Your marketing efforts should then produce ample engagement possibilities leading to the third consideration—determining which cases to accept. Fourth, after screening your opportunities, you must finalize your engagement of the cases you decide to accept, and fifth, you need to make appropriate fee arrangements. The following sections discuss these five steps.

REQUISITES OF A SUCCESSFUL CONSULTING PRACTICE

Before you can expect to effectively market and develop your practice you must first establish a solid base of operation. You will begin with the composite of who you are and what you have to offer. Once you have thought about the following key requisites and made the appropriate decisions, you will be properly prepared to venture forward with your marketing efforts.

- *Organizational Plan.* You must start with a basic plan. What is it you want to do in your practice? What will be the mix of teaching, consulting, giving testimony, and other aspects of your practice? For example, do you desire to provide primarily advice and recommendations to lawyers and others on your subject matter, or are you interested in providing expert testimony as well? Will you work by yourself or establish a staff? Will you incur the expense of an office or operate out of your home? What are your income goals? How wide a geographical area are you willing to cover? How hard do you want to work? You must ask and answer these questions to establish a basic organizational plan.
- *Market Niche.* Once you have a basic concept, your next step is to carve out a niche. Frequently, a specific or innovative niche will enhance your chances for quicker success by eliminating competitive pressures. However, you must be careful not to configure your operations so narrowly that your market is unreasonably limited. Your market niche may evolve from serving a geographical area that others are not serving, providing a specific expertise that others are not providing, offering broader services than others provide, using innovative pricing methods, or delineating any combination of factors to make you stand out in the crowd. Being in some way unique or different requires creative thinking, planning, and preparation.
- *Method of Operation.* You must be prepared to discuss your services, your fees, your procedures, and other matters before taking an engagement.
- *Reputation.* The importance of reputation cannot be overlooked. Not only is it necessary for effective marketing efforts but it also is the foundation for successful referrals.

Professionalism is a key ingredient to establishing a good reputation. Work hard at being professional in your day-to-day operations, your work product, your dealings with other professionals, and in the courtroom. The minute you begin functioning as a consultant/expert witness you are building your reputation, so make it a good one. Reputations, like a leopard's spots, stay with you once established.

MARKETING YOUR AVAILABILITY

Once you have formulated your operation base, you are in a position to market your practice or services effectively with appropriate marketing methods or tools.

Marketing Methods

Fortunately there are many ways to promote your expertise and availability. It is up to you to determine what works for you and your market area. The following methods have been used successfully by consultants/experts. You can use them all or any combination that fits your needs and purposes.

Direct Mail. This approach is frequently used. Although I have not used this method to develop my consulting/expert witness work, in my capacity as a practicing attorney I receive at least one direct mailing each week from economists, chiropractors, accident reconstructionists, engineers, investigators, and others looking to develop their practices. Direct mail really can be effective since it is a quick, relatively inexpensive, focused, and efficient method of promotion. Your target market should be attorneys lists that can be obtained from the local bar associations. If none are available, you can use the telephone directory to create your own list. Attorneys are always seeking experts located as nearby as possible to curtail travel costs, telephone bills, and other expenses. So, begin with your local area and nearby cities. Most attorneys maintain a folder or file on experts for future reference so chances are your mailing will be retained. Occasionally, you will hit it lucky and find an attorney who is seeking an expert in your area at the very moment the mailing arrives. More frequently, your mailing will be retained for future reference.

The nature of mailings can vary considerably. Our firm has received everything from brief letters to lavish brochures. Recently we received a **curriculum vitae** enclosed with a cover letter. From a lawyer's perspective, the format probably doesn't make much difference as long as the sender specifies areas of expertise and includes some credentials. This will be enough at least to warrant a telephone inquiry when the need arises. Exhibit 3-1 is an example of a mailing with curriculum vitae, whereas Exhibit 3-2 presents a brief letter that includes very little detailed information but invites inquiry. In view of the time constraints facing attorneys and the need for immediate information, I recommend that you include sufficient information to develop an interest rather than to require a response for any meaningful details. However, avoid excessive detail since that unnecessarily elevates printing and mailing expense and is "informational overkill" at the direct mailing stage.

Advertising. The advertising medium can successfully promote a consulting/expert witness practice. Whether it will work for you depends on many factors. To make a proper decision, you will want to weigh the cost against the potential return. If you decide to advertise, you must make many other decisions. For example:

1. What geographical area should you cover?
2. Do you focus on lawyers, insurance companies, or the community at large?
3. Do you advertise daily, weekly, monthly, or occasionally?
4. What medium should be utilized? Television? Radio? Newspaper? Trade publications?

EXHIBIT 3-1 (Part 1)
Direct mail solicitation—cover letter

Veitch and Associates
111 West Olmos
San Antonio, Texas 78212

Dear Sir:

I am writing to let you know of the service in the field of traffic accident reconstruction I can provide. Below is a partial list of the services. I am a full-time Houston policeman and provide this service on my off-duty time.

Please let me know if I can be of any service to you or if you would like any additional information.

Attached is my resume.

Traffic Accident Analyst and Reconstruction Service

—Scale Diagrams
—Demonstrative Aids
—Photography
—Expert Witness Testimony

My fee for the above services is fifty dollars ($50.00) an hour plus a seventy-five dollar ($75.00) administrative fee and all expenses incurred at my cost.

Sincerely yours,

Ima Investigator

Enclosure

EXHIBIT 3-1 (Part 2)
Expert resume

Birth: Houston, Texas
January 1, 1947

Graduate of All America High School, Class of 1966

Served in the United States Army from January 1967 to January 1969. I worked directly under the Provost Marshal as military police liaison to the Republic of Espanola.

Entered the Houston Police Department in September 1969. I was assigned to the Patrol Division from 1969 to 1982. Some of the special duties I performed other than the routine day-to-day normal police duties were field training officer, city mayor driver, and hostage negotiator.

In 1982, I transferred to the Traffic Division. From 1982 to 1984, I was assigned to the Houston Freeway System. Duties also included traffic and crowd control at the different functions throughout the city as well as traffic accident investigation and motor vehicle law enforcement.

From 1984 to the current time I have been assigned to the Traffic Investigation Unit. Duties are follow-up investigation on traffic fatality accidents and filing cases of involuntary manslaughter, criminal negligent homicide, and failure to stop and render aid with the District Attorney's office; follow-up investigation on all hit-and-run traffic accidents; the filing of class "B" misdemeanor and fleeing-the-scene cases with the District Attorney's office.

I have made on-the-scene investigation of several thousand traffic accidents. I have made on-the-scene and follow-up investigation on more than 75 traffic fatal accidents. I have assisted in the follow-up investigation of more than 50 traffic fatal accidents.

On each of the past three years I have received 40 hours of in-service school. The in-service school normally includes updates on tactics and current changes in the law. This past year, I received an eight-hour course on vehicle occupant safety.

EXHIBIT 3-1 (Part 2) *(continued)*

In June 1985, I successfully completed a 40-hour course in Advanced Traffic Accident Investigation at Brainy Junior College.

In June 1986, I successfully completed an 80-hour course in Traffic Accident Reconstruction at Podunk University.

In March 1988, I successfully completed a 40-hour course in Motorcycle Accident Investigation from Podunk University.

In September 1989, I successfully completed an 80-hour course in Advanced Accident Investigation in Houston, Texas, from Podunk University.

EXHIBIT 3-1 (Part 3)
Areas of study

1. Vehicle lamp evaluation
2. Vehicle lamp analysis
3. Tire damage
4. Photogrammetry
5. Human factors
6. Vehicle dynamics
7. Vehicle damage evaluation
8. Measuring and diagramming
9. Time and distance
10. Speed equations
11. Vault speed equations
12. Combined speed equations
13. Linear momentum
14. Weight shift equations
15. Roadway physical evidence
16. Falls, vaults, and flips
17. Vehicle kinetic energy
18. Motorcycle speed estimates
19. Critical speed equations
20. Quadratic equations
21. Formula derivation
22. Collision damage estimates

EXHIBIT 3-2
A brief direct mail letter

ARNOLD APPRAISER
& COMPANY, INC.

Dear Attorney:

I thought you might be interested in reading the enclosed business valuation article that I wrote with Victor Valuator.

Our firm has been providing business appraisals and fairness opinions to companies and individuals for over seven years. Most of the appraisals have involved some form of litigation, and as such, we have also satisfied the client's needs by additionally providing expert testimony when required.

Our appraisals and testimony have been successfully utilized in addressing valuation issues in the Federal Bankruptcy and Tax Courts as well as State Courts.

If you or your clients would like to inquire into our business appraisal services and how they may be of help to you, please call so we may either visit over the phone or set up a meeting during which we can answer your questions. Should you wish for references we will be glad to furnish these as well.

Very truly yours,

Arnold Appraiser

AA/sma

The answers to these and other pertinent questions will depend largely on your own circumstances. Because of the specialization of consulting/expert witness knowledge, however, you should usually choose a focused "rifle shot" approach. Television, newspaper, radio, and similar approaches are often unduly broad and wasteful in comparison with trade journals. Determine where most of your business will come from and direct your attention accordingly. Generally, lawyers, insurance personnel, and members of the industry of your specialty will be the sources of business.

Once you have determined how wide a geographical market you want to work in, contact lawyers and insurance personnel and find out what publications they regularly read and review. Another guideline is to find out their sources for locating experts.

You can expect to be judged and measured by your advertisements since they are a preview of yourself. So, be careful and use good taste. Remember that assertions or statements made in your advertisements are available to the cross-examiner. See Exhibit 3-3 for a sample brief ad that I have used in years past.

EXHIBIT 3-3
A sample brief advertisement

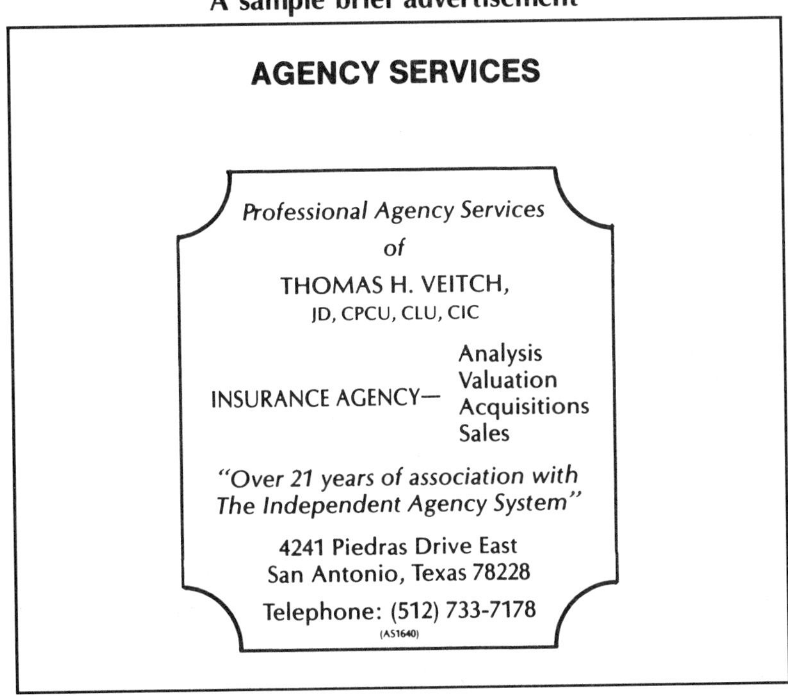

Speeches and Seminars. Lectures, seminars, speeches, teaching of classes, and other forms of verbal presentations are highly successful methods of developing your reputation and business base. Coincidentally, public speaking also tends to develop your verbal presentation skills and subject knowledge. Assuming that you are adequately prepared and develop good verbal communication skills, you will be amazed at how quickly this method can help you promote your reputation and business. It is a prime practice builder.

Whether you focus on speeches, teaching, or seminars depends on personal preferences as well as available opportunities. Be on the alert for speaking and teaching engagements. Initially, you may need to consider whatever comes along and let that exposure help you cultivate better opportunities.

Seminars may be harder work and more costly, especially if you have to go it alone. However, your own seminar may also give you more latitude and can produce quick results. If you do decide to put on some seminars, make sure you handle them properly. If you create the wrong impressions, it may be difficult ever to reverse them. Many publications are available on the proper planning and presentation of seminars to serve as a resource guide.

Written Publications. Books, articles, and other written publications are a solid way to create recognition and respect for your professional knowledge and expertise. In addition to conveying knowledge to others, your publications provide a constant reminder of your professional expertise.

Articles in trade journals and similar publications can be as easy or complex as you want to make them. Generally, the simpler the article, the quicker you can write it and the more prolific you can be. An abundance of quick, concise articles will provide broader coverage quickly. On the other hand, a well-written in-depth article, in addition to imparting important knowledge, commands respect and can lead to good, solid opportunities.

Although writing a book is not for everyone, such a comprehensive undertaking can only multiply your opportunities as an expert witness. Be certain, however, that you have the time, knowledge, and determination to complete the project before you get in the middle of something you may live to regret.

Brochures and Newsletters. I recommend these tools highly. They are relatively inexpensive and can be easily focused on your target market.

Although there are many newsletter services available, write your own, if possible. Since we are all inundated with mailings, including many polished newsletters from insurance agents, real estate agents, and others, a concise, personalized, newsletter is much more effective and has a better chance of being read. I have used the format shown in Exhibit 3-4 for several years with very good results and excellent feedback.

A nice thing about newsletters is that you can target them to a key network of clients, friends, or referral sources. They enable you to keep in touch with prospects without constant follow-up.

> *Practice Tip:* **The key is to keep the newsletter short, readable, and informative. Be sure to update your mailing list by recording address or firm name changes as you are informed of them.**

Brochures have the advantage of being able to put a summary of your services and credentials in someone's hand right on the spot. I often use the brochure in lieu of a business card. It gives a more lasting impression and provides more information. Exhibit 3-5 shows a format that I have utilized successfully for many years.

You can fold the brochures lengthwise and carry them in your jacket pocket for ready access and handout. As with the newsletter, I recommend that you create and write your own brochure to convey your own personal message and style. This approach also will save you some money. However, since it conveys

EXHIBIT 3-4
A sample "letter" newsletter

VEITCH & DAVIS

Lawyers

A PARTNERSHIP INCLUDING PROFESSIONAL CORPORATIONS

*THOMAS H. VEITCH, CPCU, CLU, CIC
JOHN H. DAVIS

DANE PATRICK

111 W. OLMOS DRIVE
SAN ANTONIO, TEXAS 78212
(512) 829-7183
FAX (512) 829-0734

OF-COUNSEL

J. DAVID BROWN

INSURANCE LAW NEWSLETTER
July, 1991

Dear Clients and Friends,

While we appear to be emerging from the "abyss" relative to problems of war and recession, the insurance arena continues to be tumultuous. The following presents some current items of significance.

TWELVE POINTS CONSIDERED BY INSURANCE COMPANIES IN EVALUATING CLAIMS

(1) OPPOSING COUNSEL - Experience, reputation, track record.

(2) VENUE - Where will the case be tried? How liberal are the jury's? What has been the verdict history?

(3) THE TRIAL COURT - What are the characteristics and propensities of the trial court? Does the Judge have a defendant's or plaintiff's background?

(4) THE PLAINTIFF - Consideration should be given to age, nationality, background, education, employment history, stability, past history for injuries, general appearance and demeanor and similar matters.

(5) THE DEFENDANT - Basically the same considerations as for plaintiff. In addition, reputation and co-operativeness are very important.

(6) THE WITNESS - How many - reputation and credibility.

(7) LIABILITY - Is there clear liability? What are the facts?

(8) DAMAGES - How extensive? How believable? How provable? Are there any inflammatory elements to the case. What are the punitive damage considerations?

(9) DEFENSES AND APPLICABLE LAW - Is there any comparative fault? Are there co-defendants? What defenses are applicable? How clear are the issues?

*BOARD CERTIFIED IN ESTATE PLANNING & PROBATE LAW
TEXAS BOARD OF LEGAL SPECIALIZATION

EXHIBIT 3-4 *(continued)*

INSURANCE LAW NEWSLETTER **Page 2**

(10) INSURANCE COVERAGE - What are the limits? How clear is the coverage? What are the settlement possibilities? Has the insured complied with policy requirements?

(11) SUBROGATION - Is it viable? Are the subrogation rights intact?

(12) COST OF LITIGATION - How much will it cost? How long will it take?

CASE LAW UPDATE

(1) BAD FAITH - A recent Corpus Christi opinion clarified that a mere difference of opinion, as to reasonable interpretations of what the insurance policy says, is no basis for "bad faith" damages. Automobile Insurance Co. of Hartford v. Davila, 805 S.W.2d 897.

(2) UNINSURED/UNDERINSURED MOTORISTS - While insurors frequently refuse to pay policy benefits if the insured has settled with the third-party without the insurors consent, a recent Alabama Supreme Court case indicates a possible national trend to the contrary. Lambert v. State Farm, No.89-1098 (Alabama, January 25, 1991).

(3) NO REASONABLE BASIS FOR CLAIM DENIAL - The Insuror denied a claim for theft of a four wheeler under a homeowners policy. The court found that the insuror failed to perform a investigation to support their position and did not seek a legal opinion until after the erroneous denial. Beacon National Insurance Co. v. Reynolds, 799 S.W.2d 390.

(4) POLICY INTERPRETATION - The determination of whether the provisions of an insurance policy are ambiguous is a question of law for the Judge. If the Judge decides the policy is ambiguous, then questions of fact are submitted to the jury as to the meaning of the policy language. Gualden v. Johnson, 801 S.W.2d 561.

(5) EXPERIENCE RATING - A very recent decision held that the insured was not liable for additional premiums based on SBI experience rating of a CGL policy where the policy language provided that "all premiums were to be completed in accordance with the companies rules and regulations (not the SBI)". The insurance company tried to collect after the policy was already cancelled. National Union Fire Insurance Co. v. Clemter, 807 S.W.2d 824

Please do not hesitate to call if we can provide any clarification or further information on these matters.

Very Truly Yours,

Thomas H. Veitch

EXHIBIT 3-5
A professional brochure

VEITCH & DAVIS

Lawyers

111 W. Olmos Drive
San Antonio, Texas 78212
(512) 829-7183

THOMAS H. VEITCH

Graduated from St. Mary's School of Law in 1973. Tom has been associated with the insurance business for over 25 years starting as a claims adjuster in 1963. He has written articles and given lectures on many aspects of insurance, probate, and tort law. In addition to belonging to a number of local, state and national bar associations, Tom has attained the CPCU, CLU, and CIC insurance professional designations.

JOHN H. DAVIS

Graduated from St. Mary's School of Law in 1968. John has over 20 years experience in the litigation of civil trials in Texas courts. He is a member of the Texas Trial Lawyers Association, San Antonio Bar Association, and State Bar of Texas.

EXHIBIT 3-5 *(continued)*

WHAT WE CAN DO FOR YOU...

ACCIDENT and INJURY CASES: We have broad experience representing both insurance companies and individuals in a variety of tort lawsuits ranging from auto accidents to worker's compensation.

INSURANCE LAW: Our firm engages in all types of insurance cases including liability, life, health, fire, disability, and miscellaneous forms of property insurance.

WILL CONTESTS and ESTATE ADMINISTRATION: We work with the family or Executor to settle the Estate. This includes accounting for all assets, payment of debts, preparation of tax forms and distribution of assets. We also handle guardianships, will contests, and other contested probate cases.

BUSINESS LAW: Incorporations, partnerships, business contracts, non-compete agreements, and sales and purchases of businesses are the types of business matters we handle on a regular basis.

ESTATE PLANNING, WILLS and TRUSTS: No estate is too large or small for consideration whether it involves intricate tax planning or simple document preparation.

OTHER MATTERS: We will endeavor to serve your personal, family, and business needs. When you have a legal matter that we do not handle we will gladly refer you to a lawyer experienced in that area.

THOMAS H. VEITCH is Board Certified in Estate Planning and Probate Law but is not certified in any other area by the Texas Board of Legal Specialization.

JOHN H. DAVIS is not certified by the Texas Board of Legal Specialization.

ABOUT OUR FIRM...

The law firm originated in 1974 and engages in a general civil law practice. Our objective is to maintain a law center large enough to fulfill our clients' needs yet small enough to provide personalized prompt service for our clients.

OUR OFFICES...

We acquired our office building in 1986. Our central location in the Olmos Park area and convenient on site parking facilitate office visits.

LEGAL ASSISTANTS...

DENISE BYLER is our Office Administrator. She has been with us since 1985 and is a candidate for the Associate Degree as a Paralegal at San Antonio College.

TINA HENDRIX obtained her Paralegal degree in 1987 at San Antonio College. Tina handles a variety of complex tasks for our clients.

your professional image, you will want to devote the same degree of preparation and dedication to detail as you would in preparing to serve as an expert witness. Exhibit 3-6 provides a summary and rating of the various marketing methods available to the expert witness-consultant.

EXHIBIT 3-6
An all-star summary of marketing methods*

Description of Method	*Rating*	*Comments*
Direct mail	***	The success of direct mailing depends on how effectively you target your market.
Advertising		
Television	*	Not really applicable.
Radio	*	Not really applicable.
Newspaper	**	Not really applicable.
Trade publications	***	Very useful, but you need to stay with it for the long run.
Listings	***	Contact Bar Association offices for potential sources.
Yellow pages	**	List under Attorneys' Services as well as your profession.
Billboards	*	Not really applicable.
Oral communication		Any and all of these methods can be very effective.
Speeches	****	
Seminars	****	
Teaching	*****	
Written publications		
Books	****	
Articles	****	
Technical papers	****	
News column	*****	
Brochures	****	
Newsletters	*****	

*5 stars designates highest and best use.

The Curriculum Vitae

Your **curriculum vitae** serves two purposes. First, it is a method of marketing yourself to lawyers and other prospective clients. Second, it provides a method of detailing your background and credentials in cases in which you testify.

"Curriculum vitae" is really nothing more than a fancy name for professional resume. Personally, I prefer the latter term since it is less pretentious and seems to relate better with a jury. Many professional resume services are available, but I once again recommend that you prepare your own. Knowing how to communicate and write effectively is essential for a successful expert witness. Therefore, you probably have the ability to create as good a product as you would purchase, and perhaps better.

If you still have your college resume, you can start with that and add to it to bring it up to date. The example shown in Exhibit 3-7 is a resume that I have maintained and updated annually for the past 30 years. If you are uncomfortable with presenting a resume with all your personal background to the jury, you can prepare a second and more concise resume detailing your credentials for use in cases where you will be testifying.

You will note that the sample resume combines legal experience and insurance experience into one resume since they dovetail for expert witness or legal representation purposes. However, if you intend to provide expert witness services in more than one area of expertise, it may be advisable to prepare separate resumes for each discipline. Once you get your resumes on the word processor, it's a snap to update them each year. To help you remember to do this, make it one of your New Year's projects each January.

SCREENING THE ENGAGEMENT POSSIBILITIES

After you have successfully applied the methods discussed in the previous section, you are likely to receive ample offers of engagement opportunities, if that is not already the case.

EXHIBIT 3-7
Professional resume

NAME	THOMAS H. VEITCH, JD, CPCU, CLU, CIC
ADDRESS AND PHONE	Personal: 111 Arrow Mound (Shavano Park) San Antonio, Texas 78231 Telephone: (512) 492-3271 Business: Veitch & Associates A Professional Corporation 111 West Olmos Drive San Antonio, Texas 78212 Telephone: (512) 829-7183
PERSONAL BACKGROUND	Married to Anne C. Veitch with five children ranging in age from 19 to 30. Born June 9, 1938, and raised in Lake Odessa, Michigan. Served in U.S. Army Reserves and honorably discharged in July of 1972.
EDUCATION	*St. Mary's University School of Law.* Graduated in May 1973, ranked in top 10% of total student body (13th in class of 152). Academic Honors included Dean's List, and American Jurisprudence Awards for top class grades in Labor Law and Equity. *Central Michigan University (1956–1960).* Received Bachelor of Science Degree in June 1960. Majored in Business Administration with minors in Economics and Geography. *Other Academic Achievements:* 1. Received Chartered Life Underwriter (CLU) designation in September 1975. 2. Received Chartered Property Casualty Underwriter (CPCU) designation in 1970. 3. Inactive candidate for Masters Degree in financial planning—American College Graduate School of Financial Sciences—18 hours completed.

EXHIBIT 3-7 *(continued)*

4. Received Certified Insurance Counselors (CIC) designation in July 1983.
5. Received Certification by Texas Board of Legal Specialization in Estate Planning & Probate Law, January 1985.

EMPLOYMENT Engaged in the practice of law since 1973, in San Antonio, Texas. The firm of Veitch & Associates conducts a general practice in Civil and Trial law. Personal practice focuses on Insurance Claims, Wills, Trusts, and Probate Law, and Automobile Accident Cases.

Previously employed by Atlantic Insurance Companies (45 Wall Street, New York, New York) in various management positions from 1967 to 1973.

Prior insurance business interest in Commercial Underwriters Agency, San Antonio, Texas (Founding Partner) from 1981 to 1984.

Total experience in insurance business spans more than 25 years and encompasses experience in claims adjusting, underwriting, sales and field management positions, insurance defense work and agency consultation in mergers and acquisitions, valuations, and similar business law matters.

FRATERNITIES Phi Sigma Epsilon, Social Fraternity and Phi Delta Phi, Legal Fraternity.

SOCIAL AND CIVIC ACTIVITIES AND MEMBERSHIPS Boy Scouts of America—served as Activities Chairman, District I, Alamo Council, 1974.

Nominated to Who's Who in Texas (1974 and 1985).

Past President of Oak Hills Lions Club.

Member of Masonic Lodge A.F. & A.M. and Scottish Rite.

Selective Service Board Member (Local Board 113—1981 to present).

EXHIBIT 3-7 *(continued)*

Nominated to Who's Who in San Antonio (1985).

Christ Episcopal Church—Active member.

Northside Chamber of Commerce—Member 1983–1986. Greater San Antonio Chamber of Commerce—Member 1987 to present.

City of Shavano Park—Former Councilman and Mayor Pro-tem; also served as member of water board and Assistant City Attorney. Currently serving on Planning and Zoning Commission.

SABOR Toastmasters—Member, 1986 to present (served as President, Vice President, and Secretary-Treasurer. Business and Professional Toastmasters Club Member.

The Plaza Club.

Fair Oaks Country Club.

San Antonio Rotary Club.

Concord Athletic Club.

The Lamplighters Dance Club.

PROFESSIONAL ACTIVITIES AND MEMBERSHIPS

INSURANCE AND FINANCIAL

Honorable Order of Blue Goose (Insurance Social Organization) member and Past President (elected Gander of the Year in 1974).

Chartered Life Underwriters CLU—Past Chairman of Bylaw Committee.

San Antonio Board of Realtors—Member and lecturer 1980–1986.

Chartered Property Casualty Underwriters, Past President of Alamo Chapter (1974).

Part time instructor of Insurance Classes at San Antonio College, also Life Insurance Law, Estate Planning and Business Planning (1972–1982).

EXHIBIT 3-7 *(continued)*

Associate Adjunct Faculty—College for Financial Planning, Denver, Colorado (1981–1983).

Nominated to Who's Who in American Insurance (Charter Edition).

San Antonio Independent Insurance Agents Association. Served as Director and Chairman of Education Committee (1983 and 1984).

International Association of Financial Planners—Served as Vice President of Education for San Antonio Chapter (1983–1984).

Nationwide lecturer on Insurance, Estate Planning and Business Law subjects for Insurance Achievement of Baton Rouge, Louisiana (1974–1980).

LEGAL

Texas Bar Association.

American Bar Association.

San Antonio Bar Association.

San Antonio Estate Planners Council.

San Antonio Probate Law Association.

Texas Association of Defense Counsel (1978–1986).

San Antonio Bar Foundation.

Diplomate Court Practice Institute.

Admitted to Western District of Texas of United States District Court.

Admitted to United States Court of Appeals, Fifth Circuit.

Admitted to U.S. Supreme Court.

Ten plus years as member of Property Insurance Committee of American Bar Association.

Past Chairman of Supervising Law Students Committee—San Antonio Bar Association.

Past Chairman—Lawyer Referral Committee—San Antonio Bar Association.

EXHIBIT 3-7 *(continued)*

	Past Member of State Bar Committee for "Alternate Methods of Resolving Disputes."
	Past Member of State Bar of Texas Committee on Professional Competence.
	Served as Vice Chairman of State Bar of Texas Committee on Prepaid Legal Insurance.
	Nominated to Who's Who in American Law (1985).
PUBLICATIONS	"Obligations of the Insured after Incurring a Property Loss" (INCL Brief March 1980, published by the American Bar Association).
	"Current Developments Involved in Incorporating an Insurance Agency" (*The Insurance Record,* April 3, 1980, Vol. XLVI, No. 7).
	Author of a concentrated Study Course and outline for CPCU, Part 1, published by Insurance Achievement of Baton Rouge, Louisiana (1975).
	"Estate Planning Considerations for the Independent Insurance Agent" (*The Insurance Record,* September 15, 1982, Vol. XLIX, No. 19).
	"Property Insurance Considerations for the Practicing Attorney" (*Texas Bar Journal,* April 1984).
	"Non-Compete Covenants" (*Texas Insuror,* May–June 1984).
	"Bankrupt Clients?" (*Texas Insuror,* Jan.–Feb. 1987).
	Authored book entitled *What You Need to Know to Settle With Insurance Companies*, published by James Publishing Group, 1991.
HOBBIES AND INTERESTS	Reading, jogging, basketball, traveling and studying Spanish (intermediate level) and German (beginning level).

The next step is to determine which opportunities to accept. Even if you are starving for business, you cannot afford to take everything that "comes down the pike." First and foremost, you will want to avoid being involved in anything that will tarnish your reputation. Second, you cannot afford to be involved in many efforts that do not provide prompt payment for your services. Economically speaking, it doesn't matter how much work you have to do if you are not being paid for it.

When it comes to trying to decide which cases to accept, the following timeworn adages come to mind:

> You can't wear two hats at once.
> You can't be in more than one place at the same time.
> No one knows everything about everything.
> You can't be all things to all people.

These adages stress that there is a limit on your knowledge as well as on your time. It is up to you to commit and apply both where they can serve you best. In making this determination, you need to consider the following questions:

Do You Fit the Case?

First, you will need to obtain a general summary of what the case is all about. Based on this, you can begin a preliminary mental evaluation of whether the case fits you and whether your opinion would support the client's position. Sometimes you will be able to determine on very sketchy facts that the case does not fit you. In other instances, you will have to probe for enough facts to decide whether you should accept or reject the offer. If you are an experienced expert witness, you should be able to isolate the issues relatively quickly and determine whether you have the appropriate qualifications to deal with the case issues.

Not long ago, I was contacted by an attorney seeking an expert witness in a **bad faith** insurance case against a life insurance company for failure to pay a claim. As I elicited information from the attorney, it became apparent that what he really needed was a person with recent day-to-day experience in examining life insurance claims. While I have extensive experience in all the collateral matters in the case and could undoubtedly have been helpful, in certain areas of testimony I did not have specific experience on the issue really at the heart of the matter. Accordingly, I suggested that the attorney attempt to find someone that could more precisely fit his client's particular need.

Occasionally, you too may receive inquiries about cases where you can address some, but not all, the issues. In such cases, the attorney is probably better off seeking an expert who can handle all the questions. That is sometimes impossible, however, so two or more experts will be retained, each dealing with different facets of the case. In that situation, be sure you know which elements of the case you are being asked to handle and that you are the best qualified person for those aspects of the case.

Do You Have the Time to Take the Case?

You are the only person who can answer this question. To make that decision, however, you need sufficient information about the engagement. It is a good idea to find out as much as you can about the timing of the case right at the outset. For example:

1. How much material will you need to review?
2. How soon will you receive it?
3. How soon will a response be required?
4. When will you be deposed?
5. When is the trial date?
6. What additional assistance will be required of you?

After you obtain a feel for the timing, consult your calendar. If you are not doing so already, you should maintain a large wall calendar that allows you to see at a glance everything you have scheduled for each day and each month of the year. Of course, you will want to maintain calendars as far in the future as your bookings require. All potential trial dates, depositions, and other appointments should be reflected on the calendar. Do not forget to record any scheduled seminars, vacations, or other commitments.

After you have determined the time requirements of the case and your time availability, you will be in a position to decide whether you can or will undertake the engagement.

Do You Want the Case?

Even though you fit the case and have the time, you may have reasons for deciding to decline the engagement. The following paragraphs highlight pertinent factors for consideration.

Stress. Is the case particularly complicated? Will the time requirements be exceptionally stressful? Do you feel a little bit on edge about the case or what may be required of you?

It is important to ask yourself questions of the preceding nature to ascertain your comfort level with the case. To do our jobs and earn a living, we all must frequently do things we would rather avoid, and this necessity creates additional stress and pressure. As an independent consultant/expert witness, you have the freedom and latitude of weighing these factors in deciding which cases to accept or reject.

> ***Practice Tip:*** **Look out for cases that have substantial emotional involvement since they are sure stress producers and should probably be avoided. If you do accept the assignment, do not get caught up in the problems and emotions of the parties or other players in the case.**

Familiarity with Parties or Lawyers. How well do you know the various lawyers involved in the case? Do you know any of the parties or other witnesses in the case? Are there any factors that would make your involvement awkward or uncomfortable for you? Be alert to the effect your involvement in the case might have on the people you know. Will it affect your reputation or future business?

Competence of Counsel. Is your client's attorney a good trial lawyer? Can the lawyer protect you in the courtroom from improper or unfair examination? Does the lawyer have the skill to guide you properly in your examination so that it will be efficient and effective?

> *Practice Tip:* **If you don't feel comfortable with or about the client's lawyer, don't get involved in the case. The lawyer is your shield and lifeline to sanity in court. The performance of a weak or unscrupulous lawyer may reflect on your reputation.**

ACCEPTING THE ENGAGEMENT

Once you have successfully completed the screening process and decided to get involved in the case, you still have to do some housekeeping before you get down to the nuts and bolts of the case.

First, you will want to have your engagement confirmed in writing. Failure to do this immediately can be the basis of misunderstanding. For example, you may have the understanding, based on a telephone conversation, that you have been hired in a case that causes you to alter your work schedule and possibly even turn down other potential work assignments. Subsequently you may not hear anything further for several weeks or months, and on follow-up, you discover that you were not engaged after all. You can avoid this sort of mix-up by requesting an immediate letter of confirmation from the client or attorney. It is better to request such a letter from the client or attorney than to send a confirming letter yourself. Requiring an affirmative act by the client and/or attorney solidifies their plans and their commitment to your involvement. You can always then respond to the client's engagement letter with any clarification or additional items that you may deem necessary.

In addition to asking for the confirmation letter, you should also request an immediate retainer. As we all know, "money talks"; if you have difficulty obtaining a reasonable retainer, it may be that the client has not really finalized the decision to engage you. It could also be an indication that you may have some problems in collecting your fee in the case. The bottom line is that you don't sit idly by assuming you have been hired in a case, and even after your hiring has been confirmed, you don't do extensive work without getting paid for it. My advice is (1) get an **engagement agreement** or confirmation letter, and (2) get an advance **retainer fee**.

A second major consideration in accepting the engagement is pinpointing the scope of your assignment. Specifically, what are you agreeing to do? Usually the letter confirming your engagement will accomplish this purpose. If not, you can always address the loose ends in a response letter. Quite often, you will receive depositions, pleadings, and other documents with the confirming letter advising you what is being requested. If the letter is not clear, follow it up. The following is a partial checklist of points that should be established in writing at the outset of the case before you commence any work.

1. Define your status as a consulting expert or expert witness.
2. Determine who you are expected to report to and communicate with.
3. Establish the fee arrangement.
4. Ascertain who is paying the bill—the client or the attorney—when the bill will be paid, and how frequently you should send statements.

5. Obtain an advance retainer fee.
6. Specify what documents are being provided for review.
7. Determine whether a written report is desired and how extensive it should be.
8. Establish all reporting and work preparation deadlines.
9. Is any investigation, testing, or additional preparatory work desired or required?
10. Does the client require responses to any specific inquiries?

MAKING THE FEE ARRANGEMENT

The matter of fee arrangements is a simultaneously sensitive, yet vital, topic. Unless you just happen to be undertaking the stress, pressures, and responsibility of expert witness work as a hobby, fee setting is paramount to your economic success.

The instant you turn to the subject of fee setting, the following questions come to mind:

- How do I establish a fee arrangement?
- What do I charge?
- What is fair?

The key point is that you want to be paid what you are worth, but you do not want to lose the business opportunity by pricing yourself out of the market.

Determining a Reasonable Fee

Many factors go into the determination of a reasonable fee.

Overhead Salary Approach. If you are maintaining an office you need to itemize your fixed operating costs. Salaries of support staff, rent, equipment rentals, installment payments, supplies, insurance, and all other fixed costs should be tallied to compute your monthly fixed costs. In addition, you will want to add the gross annual salary you expect to earn for your services. For example, if you expect an annual income of $75,000 and your fixed overhead is $50,000, you will need to generate and collect at least $125,000 per year to meet your goals. You can break this approach down further to determine your daily and/or hourly rate. Thus, if you expect to work 50 weeks out of the year, five days per work week, divide $125,000 by 250 days (50 × 5) to develop a daily rate of $500. Assuming an average of eight hours per day, your minimum hourly rate will be:

$$\$125{,}000 \div 2{,}000 \text{ hours } (250 \times 8) = \$62.50$$

The foregoing calculations develop your minimum expectations leaving no margin for error. You can alleviate this exposure by adjusting your rates upward. In this scenario, for example, you might decide to adjust your rate upward by a stated percentage such as 10 percent or, alternatively, to an arbitrary amount such as $75 per hour.

Marketplace Approach. This approach focuses on the competitiveness of the marketplace as a prime factor. You should determine what others with your expertise are commonly paid. Also, be sensitive to rate variations in different parts of the country and make adjustments accordingly.

In addition to comparing the rates of other experts, you should consider what lawyers in your area charge. You may have some difficulties finding work if you charge much more than the lawyers working on the case. It is important to scout the marketplace before you start so you can be firm and consistent with the rate you settle on. Certainly, if you publish a fee schedule for general distribution, you will want to be prepared to live with your commitment. After exploring the marketplace, your fees will reflect your judgment as to what the traffic will bear.

Fee Arrangements

A variety of arrangements can be utilized in arriving at a fair and reasonable fee for the circumstances. Although the preceding discussion will assist you in determining the value of your services, any of the following methods may be useful for establishing the actual mode of payment.

Flat Fee. If it is a short assignment and you have an accurate estimate of the amount of time required, a flat fee can be arrived at by multiplying the estimated number of hours by your hourly rate and making any adjustments deemed advisable. For example, if your hourly rate is $100 and the time expenditure is anticipated to be 8 to 10 hours, you might set a flat fee of $1,000. Remember, however, that if the project takes longer than expected, your fee will be limited to the flat fee of $1,000. As can be readily observed, this approach places most of the risk on you and is not generally recommended in litigation matters, where it is often difficult to predict the time or effort that will be required.

> ***Practice Tip:*** **If you do use the flat fee method, be very specific about the precise services that you will render, and have a clear understanding with the client that any work requested beyond the specified services will require additional fee payment.**

Per Diem or Hourly Rate. The per diem approach is in effect a flat fee for each day or partial day of service.

The hourly rate can be used by itself or in conjunction with the per diem approach. In this way, your hourly rate will be charged for partial days subject to the per diem cap. If the per diem cap is set to accommodate a 10-hour day, it will generally balance out. For example, assume your hourly rate is $100 and your per diem rate is $1,000. If you charge the full per diem rate for 7 or more hours per day, you will make money whenever your day's work is less than 10 hours and will lose money any day your work requires more than 10 hours.

As is readily apparent, the flat per diem approach may produce some inequities. For this reason, I prefer the straight hourly approach whereby you are paid for the time actually expended. If you are using the straight hourly method, you should count all your time including travel time and review time. This is all time that cannot be used on other matters and, therefore, justifies compensation. However, even this approach may require some adjustments to accommodate unusual circumstances such as missed flight connections or combination business and personal travel.

Minimum Retainer plus Hourly Rate. This method requires payment of an upfront minimum retainer fee that is fully earned for your agreement and commitment to become involved in the case. The amount of the retainer will vary depending on the complexity of the case; however, it should at least be equivalent to one per diem rate, that is, a $1,000 retainer if your per diem rate is $1,000.

The fairest approach is to apply your time against the retainer and once your time in the case exceeds the retainer collected, you should bill the excess on a regular basis such as monthly. Billing more frequently than monthly is probably too cumbersome from an economic and administrative standpoint. Billing less frequently than monthly is also not recommended since it does not produce good cash flow to cover your overhead and may lead to collection problems. If your time in the case turns out to be less than the minimum fully earned retainer, no refund will be due.

Some experts, lawyers, and other professionals use varying hourly rates for different tasks. For example, it would be possible to charge one rate for work done in your office, another for travel time or fieldwork, another for deposition and courtroom time, and so forth. This determination is a business judgment on your part. However, this approach appears unduly complicated and tedious to administer. My recommendation is that you develop an appropriate hourly rate and use it across the board for all matters with all clients and cases.

Contingency Fees. In practically all circumstances, experts should not engage in contingency fee practices if they are going to be an expert witness in the case. If the degree of participation is limited solely to consulting work and trial preparation, that is a different matter. However, if you are going to be a witness, you cannot have a financial interest in the outcome of the case. Such a position not only undermines the credibility of your testimony but is probably unethical as well. Since trial lawyers are fully aware of this stricture, it should not be an issue in most instances.

Expenses

While the earlier discussion focused on compensation for services rendered, it should go without saying that your fee agreement should also provide for payment or reimbursement of all reasonable and necessary expenses you incur. Travel expenses, costs of tests or extensive investigations, and other significant expenditures should be advanced wherever possible. Failure to obtain expense advances will eventually raise havoc with your cash flow and may occasionally result in your getting stuck without reimbursement for a bill. Be certain to record and bill all miscellaneous expenses including long distance telephone, copying, fax charges, postage, express mail, storage, and other costs. These expenses should be in addition to your hourly rate or other fee charge and are, in effect, "user fees" since they are charged to the client responsible for the expense. In addition, if you pass through these "user" costs, it will help you control cash flow and overhead expense and may deter frequent alterations of your hourly rate or fee schedule.

> ***Practice Tip:*** **In some instances, you may want to collect an expense retainer in addition to a fee retainer to cover substantial charges that are expected to be incurred soon after your involvement in the case.**

Written Fee Agreements

Regardless of the fee arrangement utilized, you should always have a written confirmation of the agreement. If the agreement is straight hourly, flat fee, or otherwise simple in context, the retaining attorney will frequently confirm the arrangement in the initial assignment letter to you. See Exhibit 3-8 for an example.

In other instances, you may initiate the correspondence by sending a letter confirming a telephone inquiry. See Exhibit 3-9 for a sample letter. In this instance, the engagement is not consummated until you receive the retainer fee from the client or the client's lawyer.

Although letter confirmation of fee arrangements is perfectly acceptable and valid, there may be occasions when you would feel more comfortable with a more formal agreement. Exhibit 3-10 provides a sample form you can use in your practice.

> ***Practice Tip:*** **Whether you use a contract or letter confirmation, always have your fee arrangement confirmed in writing. Memories tend to get fuzzy with the passage of time—especially if the case is "turning sour" for your client.**

Timekeeping

Timekeeping can be characterized as the most burdensome of tasks, yet it is laden with "little lifesavers." It seems that timekeeping has become a necessary drudgery in many professional practices. Most lawyers keep time on many if not all of their cases. You will find the same is true of engineers, accountants, investigators, independent insurance adjusters, and many others, so do not feel alone in the process.

Some people seem to have difficulty in adjusting to the timekeeping process. Accounting for all your working time each day is

EXHIBIT 3-8
Confirmation of fee agreement by attorney

LAW OFFICES OF LARRY LAWYER, P.C.
111 Aaron Street
San Antonio, Texas 78231
(512)829-7183

April 29, 1992

Mr. Thomas Veitch
VEITCH & ASSOCIATES
111 W. Olmos Drive
San Antonio, Texas 78212

Re: Cause No. 00-ZZ-1234
John D. Jones
vs.
Quick Indemnity Insurance Company, et al.
Our File No. 0000

Dear Mr. Veitch:

This letter is to confirm that our office is retaining your services as a consulting expert witness at this time. As we discussed, your fee for services rendered will be as follows:

a. A $1,500.00 nonrefundable retainer, for which our client will receive credit for work performed by you, and
b. Your hourly fee will be $150.00.

It is our client's desire to keep the overall fees as reasonable as possible. Enclosed herewith please find the $1,500.00 retainer fee.

Also enclosed please find copies of the following:

1. Correspondence between our office and Quick Indemnity;
2. Our client's insurance policy with Quick Indemnity;
3. Plaintiff's Original Petition;
4. Defendants' Original Answer;
5. Defendant Quick Indemnity's Answers to Plaintiff's Interrogatories; and
6. Defendant Quick Indemnity's Responses to Plaintiff's Request for Production of Documents.

After you have had the opportunity to review these materials I look forward to hearing from you.

Sincerely,

Larry Lawyer
LL/sma

EXHIBIT 3-9
Confirmation of fee agreement by expert

[LETTERHEAD]

[DATE]

[ADDRESSED TO]

Re: Big Lawsuit

Dear Mr. Lawyer:

This letter will confirm our telephone conversation of November 10 regarding the above matter.

Enclosed is the resume of Elmer Expert, several of our brochures, and my business card.

Our fees are $150.00 per hour for general consultation, travel time, depositions, and court time, all plus usual and customary expenses.

We require a $1,500.00 advance retainer per expert, $500.00 of which is fully earned. Our minimum fee applies if our expert(s) is named. Fees for depositions must also be made payable to Elmer Expert & Associates.

I will have Mr. Expert contact you to give you an opportunity to discuss his qualifications. If you wish to hire Mr. Expert, please forward your check made payable to Elmer Expert & Associates.

Thank you and we look forward to being of service to you.

Yours truly,

EXHIBIT 3-10
Formal fee agreement

AGREEMENT FOR SERVICES

THOMAS H. VEITCH agrees to provide services in the

____

matter discussed by the undersigned and client and the client agrees to pay the following:

A. ____________________________________;

or

B. $__________ per hour for time expended, whichever is greater, plus expenses;

Responsibility to provide services will be accepted and work will begin when we receive $__________, plus the additional sum of $__________ which will be deposited in our Trust Account and used for expenses as needed.

VEITCH will not obligate client for any large expense without client's prior approval.

If and when it becomes apparent that the above amounts for fees or expenses will be expended under this Agreement, an additional sum to be set by VEITCH will be deposited by client. VEITCH has the right to cease work and keep all funds received for services if client does not make additional deposits as requested by VEITCH.

The base fee (see A. above) is a minimum fee and no part of it is refundable. All statements for fees or expenses are due and payable in Bexar County, Texas, and within ten (10) days of receipt.

VEITCH may withdraw for good cause at any time at his discretion but in such event, shall be entitled only to a reasonable fee for services already rendered.

AGENCY SERVICES OF THOMAS H. VEITCH
4241 Piedras Drive East, Suite 115
San Antonio, Texas 78228
(512) 733-7178

____
CLIENT

By: ____________________
THOMAS H. VEITCH

____
Address

Telephone: ________________

not a natural process and is something that needs to be developed and painstakingly adhered to. However, if you keep good time records, chances are you will find your income increasing, and in addition, you will be well prepared to document your fees if any questions arise. Through the years, I have found that many benefits evolve from accurate timekeeping. For example:

1. You can identify cases where you weren't properly compensated, for example, in flat fee cases.
2. It organizes your day.
3. The detailed records help you recall information about work performed or time frames as to when certain tasks were performed.
4. You can determine where your time is spent, for purposes of efficiency.
5. Timekeeping enables you to accurately represent how much time certain tasks tend to take.
6. It provides proper documentation to support your billing.

In my estimation, the results and information are well worth the extra effort. The following brief checklist may help you be a successful timekeeper.

- *Set Up a System.* Computer timekeeping systems are available, or you can set up a manual system using time slips or a daily calendar to record your time each day. As your practice grows so does your timekeeping, so make it as simple and efficient as possible for the nature of your operation.
- *Record Everything.* Keep track of your time throughout your business day. Record your lunch break, coffee breaks, bookkeeping, administrative matters, and all the time on every case you work on. This methodical timekeeping will keep you mentally attuned to recording your time so that you don't forget to record a phone call or other chargeable event. It will

also provide you with a good analysis of whether you are using your time efficiently.

- *Use Approximations.* Do not waste your time trying to count every second or minute. Approximations are okay. I recommend that you divide an hour into tenths whereby each tenth represents six minutes. Some routine procedures such as a very quick phone call can always be charged one tenth, average phone calls two or three tenths, and longer phone calls based on the approximate time expended. Don't drive yourself silly measuring minutes.
- *Keep Your Time Records by the Phone.* For many of us, a good part of an average day is spent on the telephone. Successful timekeeping therefore necessitates the recording of all phone calls. Time records that are instantly available remind and enable you to make a record while you are talking.
- *Keep Time as You Go.* Do not wait until the end of the day or week to try and re-create your time. If you record things as you do them, you save time in the long run and will be substantially more accurate.

Practice Tip: **If you have staff, consider implementing the system with everyone. It will provide better organization and enable you to charge for staff time (at an appropriate rate). While salaries vary depending on locale and experience, a fee of $20 to $25 per hour for chargeable secretarial time is not uncommon. This is really a benefit for the client since some phone calls and other routine matters can be handled by staff (at a reduced rate) rather than by you.**

Your time records will be the basis for your client billings. Unless more detail is required by the client, your billing statement may consist of the date the work is performed, the service

EXHIBIT 3-11
Sample monthly billing statement

VEITCH & ASSOCIATES
111 W. Olmos Drive
San Antonio, Texas 78212

April 17, 1990

Mr. Joe Aaron
Attorney at Law
1234 Uptown Freeway, Ste. 110
San Antonio, Texas 78555

Re: Smith Estate

01/22/90	THV	Received and reviewed letter from client and set up new file.
01/24/90	THV	Letter to Ralph Jones.
01/26/90	THV	Telephone conference with client.
02/23/90	THV	Commenced review of client file materials; read deposition of Stephanie Morrison.
02/26/90	THV	Finished review of Morrison deposition.
02/27/90	THV	Reviewed Plaintiff's Petition.
03/13/90	THV	Reviewed deposition testimony.
03/14/90	THV	Commenced review of deposition of Stephanie Morrison.
03/16/90	GK	Letter to Smith.
	THV	Reviewed Saathoff deposition.
03/19/90	THV	Reviewed deposition of Saathoff.
03/20/90	THV	Review of Saathoff deposition.
03/21/90	THV	Review of Saathoff deposition.
03/22/90	THV	Review of Saathoff deposition.
03/23/90	THV	Review of Saathoff deposition.
03/27/90	THV	Review of Saathoff deposition.

EXHIBIT 3-11 ***(continued)***

03/30/90	THV	Review of Saathoff deposition.
04/03/90	THV	Review of Saathoff deposition.
04/10/90	THV	Finished up reviewing Saathoff deposition.
04/11/90	THV	Revised client file materials.
	THV	Worked on client file review.
04/13/90	THV	Review of file materials and Estate Planners Guidelines to work on formulation of opinion.

		Amount
	For professional services rendered	$5,513.50
02/05/90	Payment - Thank you.	($2,500.00)
	Balance Due	$3,013.50

PAYMENTS RECEIVED AFTER THE 25TH ARE NOT SHOWN ON THIS BILL.

All statements for fees and/or expenses are due and payable within ten (10) days of receipt.

If statements are not paid by the 25th of the month, a late charge will be added to the statement for each month same is overdue.

rendered, the initials of the person performing the work, and the balance due. I do not recommend showing the individual time charges unless requested since it often opens the door to unnecessary nitpicking. Exhibit 3-11 shows a sample monthly billing statement.

KEY WORDS AND PHRASES

Bad faith The opposite of "good faith." Generally implying or involving actual or constructive fraud or a design to mislead another, or a neglect or refusal to fulfill some duty or some contractual obligation.

Curriculum vitae (C.V.) A professional resume setting forth background, experience, education, and other qualifications.

Engagement agreement A written fee contract.

Per diem By the day; an allowance or amount of so much per day.

Retainer fee A fee given in advance to engage services.

CHAPTER 4

Preparing the Assignment

Once you have accepted the engagement and established the fee arrangement, the next step is preparation of the assignment. This chapter discusses key considerations involved in reviewing the case and the preparation and presentation of your expert opinions to your client.

CHARACTERISTICS FOR SUCCESS

Prior to commencing your work, remind yourself of the three essential characteristics for success in every assignment: technical skills, communication skills, and integrity and credibility.

Technical Skills

You must possess and utilize the technical skills required for the assignment. Obviously, without the necessary technical skills, you don't qualify for the job. If you do not fully or properly utilize your skills, you are not doing your job. Remember the caveat expounded in the preceding chapters, "Do not accept work for which you are not fully qualified, and do not attempt to express opinions on matters that extend beyond your specific expertise." No matter how great the temptations, failure to adhere to this rule may subject you to undue embarrassment and will be damaging to your reputation.

Communication Skills

Regardless of your knowledge, expertise, and technical skills, unless you have, or develop, the ability to impart this information clearly and persuasively to the judge and jury, you will severely curtail your effectiveness as an expert witness. I am not suggesting that you have to be a showperson. You do, however, need to convey a demeanor of confidence and authority. Additionally, you must develop the ability to convey complex technical knowledge in a manner that is understandable and meaningful to the jurors. If you confuse the jurors with technical "mumbo-jumbo" or put them to sleep with a mindless monotone, you may as well not appear in the courtroom. Accordingly, it is vital that you be ever mindful of your communicative skills and how to utilize them in your presentation of each case.

Integrity and Credibility

Even if you have the appropriate technical and communicative skills for the assignment, you are still doomed to failure unless the jury is unstintingly convinced of your honesty and propriety. You must be honest to yourself and your client in all statements of opinion that you render. Never attempt to express an opinion that you do not firmly adhere to and that is not clearly supportable. If you have "chinks in your armor" the cross-examiner will attack them mercilessly and undermine your believability in the eyes of the jury.

You must at all times maintain a professional demeanor and completely convince the jury of your honesty and integrity by testifying clearly, forthrightly, and candidly.

HOW TO GET STARTED

Your job as an expert witness is to testify as to your opinions (**opinion evidence**) on selected matters. To do this, you must first know the precise issues on which to address your opinions, and secondly, you must have a complete factual background on the case to form and substantiate your opinions.

Pinpointing Your Assignment

Your initial indication of what is expected of you will come from your oral discussions with the client or the client's attorney at the outset of the case. This may be promptly followed by an assignment letter requesting certain information of you. As you proceed into the development of the case, you will undoubtedly begin to have some observations or indications of your own as to where you can be of service. Although in some matters you may be just one of several experts and engaged for a very narrow and specific purpose, that is generally not the case. For the most part, trial lawyers fully recognize the complexities of the case and welcome all the help they can get. So be as helpful and supportive as you can, but remember that the attorney is the quarterback and as such will mastermind the plan of attack. Your job is to be a 100 percent supportive team player. You can accomplish that by determining exactly what is expected of you, doing it, and doing it well.

Gathering the Facts

Obtaining all the facts is a crucial part of the process. To do your job properly, you must know the case as well as the attorney does. The tough part is that you must do it by yourself and more rapidly. Customarily, you will not have the luxury of being able to assimilate the information leisurely over several months or perhaps years. Nor will you have the opportunity to sit through deposition after deposition gleaning the information as you go. More often than not when you enter the case, time deadlines will be imminent and rigid.

You will be required to obtain and assimilate vast amounts of information rapidly and clinically. You will be required to discipline yourself to meet the pending deadlines yet concomitantly absorb information correctly and efficiently.

At the outset, the attorney will either provide selected portions of information or will ask you to advise your needs. Once you have received and perused this information, you will undoubtedly need to request additional material.

The failure to be aware of all the pertinent facts in the case can be the source of a possible change in your opinions with substantial damage to your client's case. The only way to minimize this possibility is to review the entire case thoroughly by obtaining all the facts. You must, therefore, work closely with your attorney to be certain that you receive all the pertinent data.

In addition, you may need to do some data gathering of your own either initially, or later as you prepare for the showdown.

The following is a list of the general information you may need to obtain and review in preparing your assignment:

- Correspondence
- Investigative reports
- Photos
- Test results
- Witness statements
- Police reports
- Fire Department reports
- Medical bills and reports
- Applicable documents
- Diagrams or drawings
- Corporate or business records
- Financial statements
- Case law
- Statutory law
- File notes or memoranda
- Videotapes
- Catalogs or resource materials
- Plaintiff's pleadings
- Defendant's answers
- Interrogatories
- Requests for admissions and responses thereto
- Depositions
- Other expert reports
- Newspaper or magazine clippings or articles
- Recordings

As indicated by the preceding list, the assimilated factual data and documentation may be overwhelming.

In many instances, it may be extremely helpful if the client's attorney will provide you with an index of all exhibits and documentation. In addition, a history and chronology of the case that organizes the sequence of events and provides you with a road map can be helpful. Obviously, summaries and indexes can only serve as an introductory guide to facilitate your entry into the case. Such material cannot be relied on as factually correct; you must examine the data, that is, exhibits, depositions, and so on for that determination.

Because everything provided to you for review is subject to review by the opposition once you are designated as a testifying expert in the case, many attorneys prefer simply to give you the file information without any summaries or recitations.

In fact, as often as not, you can expect to receive a box full of documentary information, accompanied by a brief transmittal letter (or no letter at all).

Evaluating the Facts

After you have gathered all the facts, you must then engage in the prodigious task of reviewing them. To accomplish this goal, you must:

1. Organize a plan of attack.
2. Set deadlines.
3. Read everything.
4. Make copious notes.
5. Conduct such additional research, investigation, or tests, as may be necessary.

Your review of the existing material should usually commence with a review of introductory or chronological information received from the client's attorney followed by a thorough perusal of the pleadings. The pleadings establish the framework of the case based on the various contentions and responses contained therein and will provide you with an immediate feel for the case.

> ***Practice Tip:*** **As you proceed in your review of the material, maintain lists of:**
>
> 1. **Additional things to do.**
> 2. **Questions for counsel.**
> 3. **Important facts and where they are found (mark the key areas in the material).**
> 4. **Your tentative theories and opinions.**

FORMULATING YOUR OPINION

After you have completed your review and evaluation of the file material, you are ready to work on the formulation of your opinion evidence. You will base your opinions on information gleaned in your file study plus any follow-up information received as a result of your discussions with counsel and any independent research, investigation, or testing you may have conducted.

The formulation of opinions is the thought-provoking aspect of the process. You simply have to think it all out and fit the puzzle together, as you see it.

If you are likely to testify in the case, you must prepare your formulation of opinions so that it will stand up in court. In other words, you must be prepared with the following:

1. Your opinions (opinion evidence).
2. The basis for your opinions.
3. The ability to identify each and every fact on which you base your opinion evidence.

The bottom line is that you must be thoroughly prepared to support your opinions. Accordingly, you do not want to espouse any opinions you cannot readily support. Your opinions may be based on:

1. Matters on which you have personal knowledge developed by observation, education, experience, or training.
2. All the assumed facts based on the testimony and documentation provided by others, including inadmissible facts, providing it is information reasonably relied on by other experts in the field (see Rule 703, Federal Rules of Evidence).

THE EXPERT'S REPORT

After formulating your opinions, you should be ready to report to your client's attorney. Generally, your initial report will be oral. The attorney will decide whether a written report is desired based on the facts and circumstances of the case. The primary drawback to the written report is that it provides a road map for the opponent's attorney in taking your deposition or cross-examination at trial. Additionally, it helps the opponents to strengthen the weak points in the case or determine areas where they need better preparation.

If a written report is requested, be sure you know whether an extensive or short form report is desired. The short form report provides a statement of your opinions and a general discussion of your findings. The extensive report, on the other hand, requires a thorough and comprehensive discussion of fact and basis of conclusions complete with attachments of applicable photographs, diagrams, test results, or other pertinent exhibits.

Lawyers occasionally desire written reports to enhance settlement discussions. If your findings, **inferences**, and **conclusions of fact** are highly favorable to the case, an extensive written report documenting that position may be just the touch needed to facilitate settlement.

On the other hand, if the case appears headed for a certain trial showdown, the attorney may be more reticent to provide the opposition with an extensive written report for the several reasons previously discussed.

From the standpoint of the expert witness, I have found that the written report is a useful tool for organizing a deposition or testimony. If no written report is requested, you will still find it necessary in most cases to maintain organized notes to assist you in the orderly presentation of your findings and conclusions of fact on the case.

While the precise format of an expert's complete written report will depend on the nature and circumstances of the case, the following items should be included in all reports:

- *Cover Sheet and Folder.* A cover sheet and folder will give your report a neat and professional appearance, and will also identify the case involved, the date, and who prepared the report.
- *Summary of Background, Education, and Experience.* This information can be included as a short preliminary section in the report, or alternatively you may include a copy of your curriculum vitae as an addendum.
- *List of Exhibits and Attachments.* Most expert's reports contain various exhibits or attachments depending on the nature of the case. A list of the exhibits and attachments serves as a checklist of enclosures and also makes it easier to review the report.
- *Statement or Description of Facts.* A recitation of the nature of the case and the basic factual considerations orients the reader and organizes the report.
- *Findings and Conclusions.* This is the crux of the report and requires a statement of your opinions along with your

findings supporting each opinion. By way of example, Exhibit 4-1 was extracted from a case involving a lawsuit by landowners against an oil company relative to rights in mineral interests and allegations of surface damage occurring in the drilling process.

> ***Practice Tip:*** **Note that in the sample report, the expert did not always provide the basis for his conclusions in the report. At deposition, however, he was examined thoroughly as to his basis for each statement. In such a circumstance, you must be able to identify the exhibit, deposition, or source for each statement or conclusion. Be prepared to support your opinions.**

- *Summary and Closing Comments.* The summary provides an opportunity to sum up and finalize the report. The summary also makes the report more professional appearing, organized, and readable.

PREPARING FOR THE SHOWDOWN

At this stage of the game, it is time to get ready for the confrontations ahead. Don't ever forget that the path to trial is a veritable jungle full of exposures and problems. Consequently, you must be as prepared as possible and must not ever think you can "wing it." The function of opposing counsel is, at a minimum, to downplay the merits of your testimony and if possible, to discredit it entirely.

Knowing Your Weak Spots

We all have strengths and weaknesses in our personalities. By the same token, your side of the case in which you are involved may

EXHIBIT 4-1
Sample statement of opinion

FINDINGS AND CONCLUSIONS

Based on the foregoing, the following are the facts, in my opinion, and the essential conclusions to be drawn therefrom:

Prior to the signing of the oil and gas lease:

1. Landman made an attempt to determine mineral interests below the surface owned by the Landowners;
2. Based on this attempt, he represented to the Landowners that their ownership constituted 191.04 mineral acres out of 276.8 surface acre ownership;
3. Landman's title search obviously was not sufficient to reach this conclusion;
4. Landman's conclusion and representation on this point was incorrect;
5. The Landowners had no particular knowledge of their mineral interest ownership, and inquired specifically of Landman about the extent of that ownership;
6. The Landowners relied on the representation by Landman as to the extent of their mineral ownership;
7. The Landowners have stated that they would not have signed the lease if Landman had represented their true mineral interest of ownership;
8. Landman probably would not have obtained other leases of the mineral estate below the Landowners' surface if he had not obtained the Landowner lease.
9. It is unlikely that any drilling on the property would have occurred if the Landowners had not signed the lease.
10. In the usual circumstances, Oilco would have learned the true extent of the Landowners' mineral interest prior to the drilling on the property, as it should have routinely had the title examined before drilling. Had that been done in this case, it would have learned then, that the Landowners' mineral interest was not the amount represented by Landman;

EXHIBIT 4-1 *(continued)*

11. Every subsequent assignee of the Landowners' working interest, beginning with Oilco, was on notice of the true extent of the Landowners' mineral interest ownership, by virtue of documents of record;
12. In February 1986, prior to the drilling on the Landowners' property, *Oilco represented the Landman's calculation of the Landowners' mineral acreage to "Operator," in its farmout agreement;*
13. In June 1986, which was also prior to drilling on the Landowners' property, "Operator" received a calculation of the same mineral interest that was substantially different from the Landowners' calculation;
14. Even in the absence of conflicting information, it is a *poor and negligent practice by the owner of a working interest, to drill oil or gas wells without examining and ascertaining precisely the state of title of the mineral interests associated with the acreage to be drilled;*
15. When drilling occurred in this case, the title to the subject mineral estate had not been properly examined by Oilco, "Operator," or any of *"Operator's" apparent partners.*
16. Prior to drilling, representatives of Longhorn Management, Inc., and their partners caused the Landowners to continue their belief that drilling should occur and that the Landowners would profit substantially from the resulting wells;

a. By representing to the Landowners that wells would be drilled at locations that would maximize the Landowners' interest in gas units;
b. By representing that the gas units would be composed of tracts that would maximize the Landowners' interest in the units;
c. By representing that the Landowners' wells would produce a substantial income;
d. By failing to disclose their knowledge of the conflicting information about the Landowners' title to the mineral interests;

EXHIBIT 4-1 *(continued)*

e. By failing to disclose that no arrangement had been made to transfer or transport the oil or gas produced to a purchaser of oil or gas, and that the granting of right of way and pipeline construction would be required.

17. It is not a proper industry practice to locate wells based solely on a location that *might benefit any interest owner,* or on the basis of a walking survey of the property;
18. Nevertheless, the foregoing was done by representatives of Longhorn Management, Inc., and their partners;
19. Drilling was performed by Longhorn Management, Inc., and its partners, through Longhorn Oil Field Construction Company, a company affiliated with Longhorn Management, Inc.;
20. The drilling of the wells was the cause of the damage to the property, with the exception of the damage incurred as the result of the granting of pipeline right of way;
21. *The manner in which the third well was drilled also constituted a use of substantially more of the property than was necessary for that purpose, and a negligent use of the same property which also contributed to the damage to the land;*
22. A representative of Longhorn Management, Inc., and its partners, again caused the Landowners to believe that they would profit substantially from the wells:
    a. By representing the necessity of granting additional pipeline right of way for the purpose of connecting the wells;
    b. By representing that the granting of such right of way was the only way to profit from the drilling of the wells.
23. Pipeline right of way was granted, pipeline construction occurred and extensive damage to the property resulted along the pipeline right of way as the result of such activity;
24. The pipeline right of way was granted to Highpeak Gas Company;

EXHIBIT 4-1 *(continued)*

25. The Landowners are entitled to their fractional interest in the royalty payable from two gas units formed incident to the two wells drilled on the property, through the date of the sale of the property.

I am preparing a calculation of the Landowners' fractional interest that is the basis on which their share of production should be paid.

SUMMARY

Taking account of all the facts, Landman erred in his title investigation and the respective defendants *were negligent in not having the title examined by an attorney prior to the drilling of the wells.* According to the Landowners, the error was a primary factor in the signing of the Landowners' lease and the drilling of the wells, and based on all the facts available, it amounted to a misstatement of facts to the Landowners on which they relied as a representation. Subsequent to misrepresentations by Longhorn Management, Inc., representations were made with regard to potential income from the wells, pooling, the formation and location of the units, and the obtaining of right of way. Taken as a whole, these events caused the *misconception of the Landowners, who believed that the drilling was being permitted by them in exchange for the benefits they would receive, i.e., substantial oil and gas income.*

also possess its weaknesses. As the case proceeds to deposition and ultimately to trial, it is essential that you be well-prepared to deal with your own personal weaknesses as well as with those in the case. For example, if you are weaker in some aspects of your area of expertise than others, try to devote additional preparation time to that part of your testimony. If you are weak in communication skills, read some books on the subject and practice giving answers to anticipated questions. Be certain that you know all the facts of the case having any bearing on your testimony and be sure that the facts on which you rely as a basis for your opinions are correct. Be aware of any weakness in your factual position since this will undoubtedly be the focus of substantial inquiry in deposition and trial. Although we cannot always excise our weaknesses, be they personal or relative to the merits of the case, we can be fully cognizant of their existence and ready to cope with them to the best of our ability. Preparedness is probably the most vital factor influencing success in lawsuits. It is, accordingly, your responsibility to "be prepared."

Assembling Your Work Products

In some cases, total preparedness will require that you conduct certain tests, inspections, or investigations. It will be up to you to determine when this is necessary and to request approval from your client to incur the necessary time and expense. In many instances, appropriate testing, investigation, or inspections will provide you with more support for your position. Even if they do not, they will help you clarify the facts and form the proper opinions. Sometimes, you may discover that your client's case unexpectedly faces some insurmountable obstacles. If this is the case, the sooner it is discovered, the better for all concerned. It is a mistake to vigorously pursue nonmeritorious lawsuits. If some bad facts develop, then your client's attorney will want to know this information as soon as possible to formulate subsequent strategy or decisions.

In some situations, testing that is destructive of evidence may be necessary. Such destructive testing may require court approval, and in any event joint consent of counsel will always be needed. Any evidence entrusted to your custody is your responsibility. Always be sure to obtain written approval prior to conducting tests, particularly destructive tests.

In some cases, an inspection of the premises or accident scene may be indicated to become more familiar with the setting. This also provides the opportunity to obtain documentation in the form of diagrams, photographs, or other information.

> ***Practice Tip:*** **When taking photographs, try to get a variety of angles to avoid any objection that the photos intentionally distort the scene in your favor. All photographs should be marked indicating the date, place, and name, address, and telephone number of the picture taker.**

Demonstrative Evidence

Demonstrative evidence can be a very useful tool for expert witnesses. Such evidence enables the expert to use more than words to convey factual information on key points. It not only clarifies the point but has substantially more impact than mere words. The following items of demonstrative evidence should be considered by expert witnesses where appropriate to the circumstances:

- Charts.
- Drawings.
- Diagrams.
- Photographs.
- Videotapes.
- Models.
- Slides.

SOME DO'S AND DON'TS

The following list summarizes the most important do's and don'ts of preparing expert witness work:

1. Don't be hesitant to research difficult and complex issues.
2. Don't rely on your attorney's memos and analysis. Do your own work.

3. Don't forget that whatever you record or reduce to writing may be discoverable.
4. Do be sure that you thoroughly digest and master all the applicable facts.
5. Do be prepared to support your opinions by applicable facts.
6. Don't conduct any tests without your attorney's consent and approval.
7. Don't testify on matters that are beyond your expertise, knowledge, or experience.
8. Do use visual aids whenever possible to illustrate key points.
9. Do attempt to make your determinations and analysis as simple and straightforward as possible to avoid juror confusion.
10. Do discuss your opinions with your client's attorney before committing anything to writing.

KEY WORDS AND PHRASES

Demonstrative evidence That evidence addressed directly to the senses without intervention of testimony. Such evidence may include maps, diagrams, photographs, models, charts, medical illustrations, X-rays.

Conclusions of fact An inference drawn from the subordinate or evidentiary facts.

Inference A process of reasoning by which a fact or proposition sought to be established is deduced as a logical consequence from other facts already proved or admitted.

Opinion evidence Evidence of what the witness thinks or believes or infers in regard to facts in dispute, as distinguished from his personal knowledge of the facts themselves.

CHAPTER 5
Depositions

Perhaps the most significant event transpiring prior to the actual trial of a case is the taking of depositions, particularly those of the various experts in the case. It is a mistake to approach the deposition procedure routinely or without being fully prepared. Many cases have been won or lost based on the results of depositions. Accordingly, it is essential that expert witnesses have a complete understanding of the deposition procedure and be prepared to give their best.

PURPOSE OF A DEPOSITION

Depositions constitute the very heart of the discovery process. As a general rule, the deposition of any witnesses, including expert witnesses, is taken by the opposing counsel. Lawyers rarely need to depose their own witnesses since they have ample uninhibited opportunity to discuss the case among themselves. However, a lawyer does not have the same access to the opposing parties or most of their witnesses. The deposition discovery procedure is widely used in all states to provide a formalized method whereby lawyers can speak with opposing parties or their witnesses. The rules of procedure provide a structure of rules governing the rights of the respective parties and witnesses in the deposition process. A discussion of federal rules governing depositions concludes this chapter.

The deposition procedure may serve any or all the following several purposes for the opposing counsel:

1. *Pin Down Your Story.* The other side wants to confine you to a prescribed story or circumstance that they can rely on for evaluating the case or for trial purposes. It will be a problem to change your testimony later; therefore, it is essential that you be fully and properly prepared at deposition.
2. *Obtain Factual Information.* The opposing counsel will want to know your opinions, observations, and all facts relied on in formulating your opinions. They will also want to discover all documents and factual information provided to you for your assignment, as well as any documentation, reports, photos, graphs, charts, diagrams, videos, recordings, or other information prepared by or for you in your advancement of the assignment.
3. *Discover Your Background and Experience.* The opponents want to know your educational background, your years of experience, how many times you have testified previously, the types of cases on which you have previously worked, the results of other cases, and many other factors that will permit an analysis of your depth of knowledge and experience.
4. *Size You Up.* Before going into the courtroom, the opposing counsel wants to know how you think and react. What is your personality type? How do you react under stress? How do you dress and groom yourself? What type of impression are you likely to make on the jury? These are all important

factors relied on by opposing counsel in evaluating the case and in preparing for your cross-examination at trial.

5. *Set You Up for Impeachment.* Discrediting your testimony or at least minimizing its impact is frequently the primary purpose of a deposition. For this reason alone, you must always be alert and wary of **entrapment.** A single lie or **misrepresentation** can undermine the **credibility** or believability of all your testimony. You can be assured that, given the chance, the opposing counsel will make the most of any impeachment opportunity and wave it before the jury like a red flag. While it is opposing counsel's job to find any weaknesses in your opinion, it is your responsibility to give them as few opportunities as possible. Refer to Chapter 7 for techniques and trick questions used by savvy lawyers in cross-examining witnesses and be prepared.

The degree of emphasis the opposing counsel directs toward each of the foregoing purposes will vary depending on the lawyer and the circumstances of the case. In some cases, the lawyer's primary objective may be to set up the case for settlement, in which case the focus at deposition will be discovering your factual information and opinions. In other instances, the lawyer may want to know how strong a witness you are going to make for case evaluation purposes. A lawyer who is focusing on preparations to litigate the case, may direct more attention to pinning down your story or setting you up for impeachment. While all the foregoing purposes are important and useful, the scope and nature of each deposition will depend on the primary purposes behind it, which can affect the questioning techniques utilized.

THE DEPOSITION PROCEDURE

A deposition is testimony under oath, much the same as if you were actually testifying in the courtroom. There are, however, several differences. Four key words frame the discussion: Who? What? When? Where?

Who Is Present?

Although the persons in attendance vary from deposition to deposition, at least four people will always be present. Assuming that the case involves only two parties, the essential attendees are the two attorneys of record, the court reporter, and the witness (deponent). If the deposition is to be video-recorded, a video technician will also be present. Additional persons in attendance could include attorneys for additional parties in the case, more than one attorney for the same party, expert witnesses for one of the other parties, or the other parties themselves. Accordingly, an average deposition may involve anywhere from four to a dozen persons and in substantial cases many more. Your attendance will generally be by agreement between the lawyers and is often formalized by a deposition notice. In those cases where counsel disagree, the deposition notice may be accompanied by a **subpoena.** In most instances, that notice will be by **Subpoena Duces Tecum** requiring you to produce certain documents at the deposition. See Exhibit 5-1 for a sample Notice Duces Tecum of intention to depose an expert witness in an insurance litigation matter.

Also of significance is *who* is *not* present at a deposition: No bailiff, no jury, and no judge are present. However, the deposition proceeds in a form and manner that anticipates the eventual revealing of the deposition testimony to a judge and jury, and is subject to procedural and evidentiary issues to be decided by the judge. Any rulings required of the judge as to the admissibility of evidence will customarily occur at the time of trial, not at the time the deposition is being taken.

What Transpires?

After the appropriate persons have assembled in the deposition room, the deposition commences. The following sequence is typical.

EXHIBIT 5-1 (Part 1)
Sample Notice Duces Tecum

Cause No. 87-ZZ-00011

VISTA VERDE, INC.	§	IN THE DISTRICT COURT
	§	
VS.	§	73RD JUDICIAL DISTRICT
	§	
AARON & AARON OF TEXAS,	§	
INC. and NORTH AMERICAN	§	
INSURANCE COMPANY	§	COMAL COUNTY, TEXAS

NOTICE DUCES TECUM OF INTENTION TO TAKE THE ORAL DEPOSITION OF THOMAS H. VEITCH

TO: THOMAS H. VEITCH
111 West Olmos
San Antonio, Texas 78212

Please take notice that pursuant to Rules 200 and 201, Texas Rules of Civil Procedure, Defendant, AARON & AARON OF TEXAS, INC., will take the oral deposition of THOMAS H. VEITCH, at the Law Offices of Smith & Moore, Twelfth Floor, ABC Bank Building, San Antonio, Texas 78205, at 8:00 o'clock A.M. on the 7th day of February, 1990. The deposition will be taken by a certified shorthand court reporter and will continue from day to day until completed. A subpoena will be issued. The subject area upon which the witness will be examined will be as follows: All facts relating to the basis for the claim of Vista Verde, Inc. asserted in this suit and the customs and practices used in the insurance industry in the bringing and selling of insurance policies.

DEFINITIONS AND INSTRUCTIONS

(a) The terms "you" and "your" shall mean THOMAS H. VEITCH, your attorneys, agents, and all other natural persons or business or legal entities acting or purporting to act for or on behalf of you whether authorized to do so or not.

(b) The term "document" shall mean writings of every kind, source, and authorship, both originals and all nonidentical copies

EXHIBIT 5-1 (Part 1) *(continued)*

thereof, in your possession, custody, or control, or known by you to exist, irrespective of whether the writing is one intended for or transmitted internally by you, or intended for or transmitted to any other person or entity, including without limitation any government agency, department, administrative entity, or personnel. The term shall include handwritten, typewritten, printed, photocopied, photographic, or recorded matter. It shall include communications in words, symbols, pictures, sound recordings, films, tapes, and information stored in, or accessible through, computer or other information storage or retrieval systems, together with the codes and/or programming instructions and other materials necessary to understand and use such systems. For purposes of illustration and not limitation, the term shall include: affidavits; agendas; agreements; analyses; announcements; bills, statements, and other records of obligations and expenditures; books; brochures; bulletins; calendars; cancelled checks, vouchers, receipts and other records of payments; charts; drawings; checkbooks; circulars; collateral files and contents; contracts; corporate by-laws; corporate charters; correspondence; credit files and contents; deeds of trust; deposit slips; diaries, drafts; files; guaranty agreements; instructions; invoices; ledgers; journals balance sheets; profit and loss statements, and other sources of financial data; letters; logs, notes, or memoranda of telephonic or face-to-face conversations; manuals; memoranda of all kinds, to and from any persons, agencies, or entities; minutes; minute books; notes; notices; parts lists; papers; press releases; printed matter (including published books, articles, speeches, and newspaper clippings); purchase orders; records; records of administrative, technical, and financial actions taken or recommended; reports of entry; schedules; security agreements; specifications; statement of bank accounts; statements, interviews; stock transfer ledger; technical and engineering reports; evaluations, advice, recommendations, commentaries, conclusions, studies, test plans, manuals, procedures, data, reports, results, and conclusions; summaries, notes, and other records and recordings of any conferences, meetings, visits, statements, interviews or telephone conversations; telegrams; teletypes and other communications sent or received; transcripts of testimony; UCC instruments; workpapers; and all other writings, the contents of which relate to, discuss, consider, or otherwise refer to the subject matter of the particular discovery requested.

EXHIBIT 5-1 (Part 1) *(continued)*

(c) "Person": The term "persons" shall include individuals, associations, partnerships, corporations, and any other type of entity or institution whether formed for business purposes or any other purposes.

(d) Unless otherwise indicated, the documents to be produced are those prepared, sent, or received during the time period from January 1, 1985, forward.

(e) As to any document that is requested for which a privilege or other protection from disclosure is asserted, be prepared to state at the time of deposition the specific ground for each such privilege or protection claimed, in order to assist the Court in determining whether or not the claim or privilege to such document is proper, and be prepared to identify the document with particularity, including its date, author, all recipients thereof, subject matter, number of pages, and the full names and job title of each person, who to the best of your knowledge and belief, have seen such document (including copies) or has knowledge of the subject matter or content.

(f) Upon producing the documents, you are requested to indicate in an appropriate manner which of the following numbered paragraphs described each of the documents produced.

PLEASE TAKE NOTICE THAT IN CONNECTION WITH THE TAKING OF THIS DEPOSITION, THOMAS H. VEITCH SHALL PRODUCE AT THE COMMENCEMENT OF THE TAKING OF THIS DEPOSITION THE MATTERS DESCRIBED IN SCHEDULE "A" ATTACHED HERETO AND INCORPORATED HEREIN BY REFERENCE.

Respectfully submitted,

____

J. WARD RANDOLPH
State Bar No. 00000234
ABC Bank Building,
12th Floor
San Antonio, Texas 78205

ATTORNEY FOR DEFENDANT,
AARON & AARON OF TEXAS, INC.

OF COUNSEL:

SMITH & MOORE

Exhibit 5-1 (Part 2)

CERTIFICATE OF SERVICE

A true and correct copy of the foregoing Notice Duces Tecum of Intention to Take the Oral Deposition of Thomas H. Veitch was served by messenger deliver, properly addressed to the following:

Mr. Leon Christian
Saathoff & Trahan
500 Sage Trail, Ste. 700
San Antonio, Texas 78231

on this ______ day of January, 1990.

____

J. WARD RANDOLPH

CERTIFICATE OF SERVICE

A true and correct copy of the foregoing Notice Duces Tecum of Intention to Take the Oral Deposition of Thomas H. Veitch was deposited in an official depository of the United States Postal Service, in a postage paid wrapper, certified mail, return receipt requested, properly addressed to the following:

Mr. David O'Donald
Greene, Rogers, & Walker
600 N.W. Loop 10, Ste. 1000
San Antonio, Texas 78216

CERTIFICATE NO.:
P 470 383 049

Mr. Thomas H. Veitch
111 W. Olmos Drive
San Antonio, Texas 78212

CERTIFICATE NO.:
P 470 383 056

on this ______ day of ____________, 1990.

____

J. WARD RANDOLPH

EXHIBIT 5-1 (Part 3)

EXHIBIT A

DOCUMENT REQUESTS

The witness is requested to bring with him to his deposition the originals of the following documents:

DOCUMENT REQUEST NO. 1:
All documents relating to Vista Verde, Inc.

DOCUMENT REQUEST NO. 2:
All documents relating to Vista Verde's claim for coverage in connection with the Incident.

DOCUMENT REQUEST NO. 3:
All documents reviewed by you and/or relied upon by you in forming your mental impressions and/or opinions concerning Vista Verde's claim for insurance coverage and/or the alleged bad faith conduct of any insurer in this litigation.

DOCUMENT REQUEST NO. 4:
Any notes or records prepared by you relating to the Incident, Vista Verde's claim for insurance coverage, and/or the alleged bad faith conduct of any insurer in this litigation.

DOCUMENT REQUEST NO. 5:
All correspondence and memoranda between you and any other person relating to the Incident, Vista Verde's claim for insurance coverage, and/or the alleged bad faith conduct of any insurer in this litigation.

DOCUMENT REQUEST NO. 6:
All documents reflecting the mental impressions and/or opinions that you have or had concerning the Incident, Vista Verde's claim for coverage, the alleged bad faith conduct of the insurers in this litigation, and/or any matter related to this litigation.

DOCUMENT REQUEST NO. 7:
All files, including the entire contents thereof, created as a result of or in connection with your engagement on behalf of Vista Verde in this and any other litigation.

DOCUMENT REQUEST NO. 8:
Your current resume.

EXHIBIT 5-1 (Part 3) *(continued)*

DOCUMENT REQUEST NO. 9:

Any and all testimonial documents, including depositions, trial transcripts and affidavits, in which you have testified concerning insurance coverage analysis, vendor's coverage, and/or bad faith conduct of insurers.

DOCUMENT REQUEST NO. 10:

All articles, speeches, and other writings by you in the area of insurance coverage, including but not limited to vendor's insurance coverage and/or bad faith conduct of insurers.

DOCUMENT REQUEST NO. 11:

Any documents tending to show that you have any expertise in the area of insurance coverage, vendor's insurance coverage, and/or bad faith conduct of insurers.

DOCUMENT REQUEST NO. 12:

Day-Time calendars and all telephone slips containing entries relating to your engagement by Vista Verde in this and any other litigation.

DOCUMENT REQUEST NO. 13:

The invoices, statements, and all backup (time slips, phone records, etc.) relating to your engagement by Vista Verde in this and any other litigation.

Sworn Testimony. You will be asked to raise your right hand and be cautioned and sworn to "tell the truth, the whole truth, and nothing but the truth," to which you should verbally respond "I do" or "I so affirm." The information you then provide will be considered to be **sworn testimony**.

Procedural Stipulations. The attorneys in the case will be asked to state or enter by writing into the record their agreements to **stipulations** as to what rules of procedure will be applicable to the deposition proceeding. The respective counsel may agree to waive the necessity of raising objections prior to trial, may agree to take the deposition pursuant to the applicable rules of procedure for that jurisdiction, or may enter into such other agreements or stipulations as are usual and customary in the applicable jurisdiction. See Exhibit 5-2 for a typical stipulation. The agreements and stipulations of counsel will govern the objections that must be voiced during the deposition and the ultimate intensity of the proceeding.

Identifying the Witness. Directly after the foregoing matters have been disposed of, you will be asked to identify yourself by stating your name into the record.

Instructions for the Witness. After your identity is established on the record, the questioning will proceed. If you have not been previously deposed, some **colloquy** may take place between you and the opposing counsel whereby you are reminded to give verbal answers (rather than nod your head or gesticulate) so that the court reporter will be able to hear and record your response. Other similar routine instructions include a reminder that your testimony can be read to the judge and jury and a request that you ask counsel to rephrase the questioning if you do not understand it. See Exhibit 5-3 for an example of typical deposition instructions. However, if you are an experienced expert witness, these instructions will often be dispensed with and the general questioning will commence immediately.

Questioning Procedure. The initial questioning will come from the attorney requesting your deposition, generally the primary opposing counsel, followed by the attorneys for the other parties in the case. The last attorney in the rotation to question you is your (client's) attorney. As a rule, your attorney will reserve any questions of you until time of trial, since he/she can always speak with you outside the presence of the court reporter and other lawyers. Obviously there is no point in giving the opposition any information they didn't ask for. Occasionally, however, your attorney will perceive some confusion or misunderstanding in your testimony and may ask a few questions to clarify the record.

EXHIBIT 5-2
Typical Deposition Stipulations

IN THE 224TH JUDICIAL DISTRICT COURT OF COMAL COUNTY, TEXAS

MADELEINE WILLIAMSON, et vir §
VS. § CASE NO. 78-ZZ-0003
JIFFY TRANSPORT, INC. and
RALPH BRITT §

APPEARANCES

Law Offices of Thomas H. Veitch
111 W. Olmos Drive
San Antonio, Texas 78212
By: Mr. Thomas H. Veitch

Benjamin Smith
Attorney at Law
2100 Bowie, Suite 1100
Houston, Texas 77002

Floyd Samuels, Sr.

Margaret Tate,
Notary Public

ORAL ANSWERS AND DEPOSITIONS of the witness Floyd Samuels, Sr., who resides in Houston, Harris County, Texas, in answer to questions propounded to him in the above styled and numbered cause, taken on behalf of the Plaintiffs, before Margaret Tate, a Notary Public in and for Bexar County, Texas, on the 17th day of April, A.D. 1980, at the Law Offices of Thomas H. Veitch, 111 West Olmos Drive, San Antonio, Texas, between the hours of 12:10 o'clock P.M. and 2:25 o'clock P.M. of said day, pursuant to the following agreement of counsel:

It is stipulated and agreed by and between counsel and the respective parties hereto, that the deposition of the witness named in caption hereto may be taken at this time and place;

EXHIBIT 5-2 *(continued)*

time and notice being waived, and that the said deposition, or any part thereof, when so taken, may be used on the trial of this case the same as if the witness were present in court and testifying in person.

It is further stipulated and agreed by and between counsel and the respective parties hereto that the necessity for preserving objections to the questions propounded or to the answers given, whether said objections go to the substance or the form of the questions or the answers, at the time of the taking of the deposition or any time thereafter, whether orally or in writing, is waived, and that any and all objections to this deposition, or any part thereof, may be made and urged for the first time at the time same is sought to be offered in evidence on the trial of this case.

It is further stipulated and agreed by and between counsel and the respective parties hereto that the witness may sign deposition before any duly authorized and acting Notary Public in the State of Texas.

EXHIBIT 5-3
Deposition Instructions

Q: Mr. Witness, if at any time you do not understand a question, I'd appreciate it if you would so indicate to me. Is that agreed, sir?

A: Sure.

Q: And after you understand the question, that you will give a full and complete and truthful answer, one that the judge and the jury can rely upon if necessary at the time of trial; is that true?

A: Yes.

Q: And have you given your deposition before?

A: Yes.

Q: You do understand, then, that you have to speak up so the court reporter can properly record?

A: Yes.

The nature of the questions to which you will be asked to respond are discussed in more detail in Chapters 6 (Direct Examination), 7 (Cross-Examination), and 8 (Some Final Tips and Thoughts).

Your File Materials. During the deposition, you may be asked to identify and testify about file documents or records. These questions may pertain to documents and records that you were asked to produce for the deposition or may consist of documents and records utilized by you in preparing for your analysis and testimony.

Generally an initial item of business will be to identify your file materials. Exhibit 5-4 is an example of questioning by opposing counsel who is trying to pin the expert down on the extent and nature of file materials.

Discussion off the Record. On occasion during a deposition, one of the attorneys may request that discussion take place off the record to clarify or resolve matters that need not be on the record or that can be discussed more expeditiously off the record.

> ***Practice Tip:*** **After returning on the record, attorneys have the right to question you on the record relative to matters that were discussed off the record. Always be careful of what you say whether on or off the record and do not volunteer anything. Limit your involvement to answering the questions truthfully and fairly.**

Signing the Deposition. After the deposition is concluded, the proceeding will be prepared in booklet form and presented to the deponent for review and signature. You will be permitted to make written note of any corrections, omissions, alterations, or additions. There is generally no requirement that your signature be notarized by the court reporter recording the deposition. It is

EXHIBIT 5-4
Sample Questions by Opposing Attorney Relative to the Experts File

Q: Would you state your name, please, sir?
A: William Witness.
Q: Mr. Witness, do you have a resume and a file on this matter?
A: I have a file.
Q: All right. Do you have a resume?
A: I do. It's one that I made up and it's updated. I haven't got it typed. Can you make a copy of it?
Q: Sure. What I'll do is ask the court reporter to attach that to your deposition as Exhibit 1, and when you come to trial, we will substitute your finalized copy for it.
A: Okay.
Q: Now, may I see your file on the matter, please?
A: (Indicating).
(At this time, a brief discussion was held off the record. Whereupon, Deposition Exhibits Nos. 1 through 15 were marked for identification.)
Q: Mr. Witness, do Exhibits 1 through 15—consisting of some 20 pages—represent your entire file on this matter except for six color photographs, which are contained in the attorney's file, and the Southwest Airlines ticket number WN-091843?
A: That's all I've really got with me now. I do have some copies of these photographs and a few other pictures that really don't show anything that mean much to me. And I've transferred all my notes really onto this paper here that I'm working from my notes for the deposition.
Q: Is that notes that you made from Exhibit 15?
A: No, it's other pieces of paper that I've made, and then I transferred them here and threw those away.
Q: So there are some pieces of paper that you have thrown away from your file.
A: Yes.
Q: There are some other photographs in Houston that are not contained in your file.
A: Right.
Q: And what else?
A: You haven't labeled my notes for the deposition.

EXHIBIT 5-4 *(continued)*

Q: Okay. Let's label those as Exhibit 16, please, sir. How many pages are there?

A: I have your name on one page, and I've just made them all on the front page here.

Q: Why did you throw those pieces of paper away and what was contained on them?

A: I threw them away because I didn't need them anymore. I had gotten all the information off them, like when my first contact was, and when I got the specimens, and when I returned the specimens, that kind of thing. My data, what it showed me, what was important, I recorded here. And my observations are also recorded here.

Q: Okay. What did you—When did you throw those pieces of paper away, Mr. Witness?

A: Yesterday.

Q: Okay. Can you—Do you still have access to them?

A: I doubt it. They probably cleaned my room by now.

Q: Okay. I'd ask that when you return to Houston you make a thorough, reasonable search and see if you can find those pieces of paper. And, if you can, I'd like to have you mail them to the court reporter for attaching to your deposition.

A: Okay.

Q: Also I would like to ask if you would make duplicates of all of the photographs that are contained in your file for me, and also duplicates of those that are not here today, and send them to me at 111 W. Olmos Drive.

A: That will be fine.

Q: Okay. Were you given any information other than what's contained in the written documents that we have here today?

A: We may have had some verbal conversations over the phone, but I never really got any new information other than what's shown here.

common for your signature to be notarized by a secretary in your office or your attorney's office.

Exhibits. Most depositions of expert witnesses involve substantial examination regarding various documents, records, or other exhibits. Some of these exhibits may relate to your file materials as discussed earlier. Other exhibits or documents are frequently presented for your review and comment at deposition. Of course, all exhibits identified and discussed at the deposition will be attached to the deposition. In those cases involving a large number of documents, the exhibits will be bound together separate from the deposition transcript itself and identified as exhibits pertaining to that deposition. On occasion, you may be asked to prepare certain diagrams, sketches, or other aids during the deposition. These items will be identified as exhibits and attached to the deposition.

Where and When Will the Deposition Take Place?

The determination of where and when varies with the circumstances of the case. However, once these issues are determined, the deposition notice (see Exhibit 5-1) will specify the time and place. Be certain that you note this information carefully as it can be rather embarrassing to arrive late for a deposition (or miss it altogether) because you were careless in reading the notice.

> ***Practice Tip:*** **It is usually a good idea to avoid depositions at your own office since it gives opposing counsel a broader access to your books and records than would be the case elsewhere where the exposure will be limited to what you have in your possession at the time.**

Although many depositions are scheduled at attorneys' offices, they are also held at the courthouse, the court reporter's facilities, your office, or various other locations dictated by circumstances.

While most depositions are scheduled to accommodate the schedules of the witnesses and various attorneys involved, this is not always possible. For example, if you are a busy physician and have been unable to accommodate the requests of counsel, don't be surprised if you receive a subpoena and notice to appear at an unexpected time and/or place. This is particularly true when the trial of the case is imminent and some depositions still have not been scheduled or taken. Rule 29 of the *Federal Rules of Civil Procedure* provides broad latitude to the parties in scheduling depositions by written stipulation. I have been involved in more than one deposition after hours while the trial was in process.

DEPOSITION QUESTIONING TECHNIQUES

As previously discussed, a variety of purposes may motivate the opposing attorney to take your deposition. The primary purpose or purposes for a particular deposition request will affect the questioning techniques utilized. Regardless of the type of examination, the onus is on the expert witness to be prepared and to listen very carefully to the questions.

Miscommunication

It is amazing how much damage or confusion can be caused by miscommunication that occurs as a result of:

1. Poorly worded questions.
2. Failure to clearly understand the question asked.
3. Failure to respond directly to the question asked.

In other words, you must not only provide carefully worded answers to the questions but also concentrate thoroughly on the wording of the question so that the question and your answer match up.

EXAMPLES

Q: (By attorney)	Did you make any efforts as Trustee to collect any interest on these notes?
A:	I did what my client asked me to do.
Attorney:	I object as nonresponsive.

In this case, the witness may have clearly understood the question, but the answer does not match up. The answer evades the question and forces the attorney to object to its nonresponsiveness.

In the following example, the witness was obviously listening closely to the wording of the question:

Q: Had you sought any legal opinion as to the meaning of the policy language?
A: No, sir, because it was not ambiguous.
Q: In your view?
A: Yes, that's the only view I can have.

Poorly worded questions are a major source of confusion and delay. Beware of questions that start as follows:

Q: Now is it my understanding, Mr. Witness, that . . . ?

It would be pretty hard to know what the attorney's understanding (or lack of it) might be. The question here was not an intent to be tricky but simply a poor choice of words by the examining attorney.

Commonly Used Questioning Methods

For deposition purposes, the questioning styles will usually consist of one, or a combination, of the following.

By the Numbers. The examiner simply plods step by step through the whole process. This commonly occurs when the examining attorney is relatively inexperienced and is relying on some sort of outline to stay on track or make sure he/she hasn't missed anything. If you get such an examiner, you're probably in for a long day.

Who Cares? This is a variation of "going by the numbers." Sometimes, however, experienced trial lawyers will throw in some unimportant questions either to get a better feel for the witness (often in an otherwise short deposition) or perhaps just to "fish" a little bit.

The Set-Up. The objective here is to proffer questions that establish a premise that may shape the next answer.

EXAMPLE

Q: Do you maintain a claim procedures manual?

A: Yes.

Q: And doesn't that manual provide guidelines for handling this type of claim?

A: Yes.

Q: And isn't it true that your handling of this claim fails to follow your own guidelines?

Random Sniping. In this scenario, the deposition proceeds in a fairly routine manner, but every once in awhile, the examiner takes a swipe at you or phrases a question in such a way as to sound intimidating.

EXAMPLE

Q: You were in favor of his having full access of the books and records of the corporation; is that what you're telling this court and jury.

NOTE: Observe how the lawyer uses a reference to the judge and jury as part of the intimidation process.

Going for the Jugular. In this scenario, the examiner focuses less on being laid back or just gathering information and places more focus on trying to pin the witness down on every point or perhaps break his/her testimony. This technique is probably not as widely used at the deposition level. Most experienced trial lawyers prefer to maintain a fairly relaxed atmosphere at deposition in hopes of getting as much information as possible; they reserve the formal style for cross-examination. This approach has the added benefit of lulling the witness into thinking there is nothing to worry about in testifying at trial.

Dealing with Objections

Although legal objections are the province of the lawyers, the savvy expert witness must be attentive to what is happening. The applicable rules of procedure and evidence provide the guidelines, subject to any agreements or stipulations by the parties.

Your main concern as an expert witness is to understand the force and effect of objections at deposition. Depending on the applicable rules, some **objections** may have to be raised at deposition. The Rules of Federal Procedure provide that all objections made at deposition as to the manner of taking it, the evidence presented, the conduct of any party, or any other objection to the proceedings shall be noted by the court reporter or other deposition officer on the deposition record. Therefore, any evidence objected to is taken subject to the objections.

Objections are voiced for many reasons in addition to compliance with procedural rules. Many times, objections are raised simply to clarify the questioning or to alert the witness to the importance of the question and to allow time for thinking about it. Some lawyers raise objections just to throw the other lawyer off stride when he/she seems to be "getting on a roll."

In any event, being attuned to the objection procedure will enable you to be better prepared for the deposition experience.

> ***Practice Tip:*** **If an objection is raised, stop talking immediately and let the lawyers sort it out. But, listen to what they are saying and be guided accordingly.**
>
> **Here is an example of a typical objection at a deposition:**
>
> > **I'm going to object to the form of that question, because it's so convoluted that it's unintelligible. I think it presumes things which certainly—it presumes knowledge that Mr. Sweatt has not testified that he had, and requires him to speculate on the mental processes that Mr. Mehringer may have been going through.**

PREPARING FOR YOUR DEPOSITION

After reading the discussion up to this point, you should recognize why preparing for your deposition is so important. You should consider all the following factors during your preparation:

1. *Review the Pleadings.* Since the pleadings tell the story and set up the issues, it is important to have them fresh in your mind.
2. *Review Your File Materials.* As discussed earlier, you will be examined about your file materials. So, know what is there, get rid of what is not supposed to be there, and be ready to discuss or explain both.
3. *Background Information.* Be prepared to detail your background, qualifications, honors, achievements, and experience.

4. *Fee Arrangement.* Be prepared to discuss your expenses and fee arrangement in the case. Review your time records, expenses incurred, and other work notations. Unless the deposition notice requires you to produce them, you may want to leave your timekeeping and accounting records with the bookkeeper to avoid undue delay and fishing expeditions.
5. *Documentation.* Be prepared to itemize all documentation and information on which you base your opinions.
6. *Assumptions and Opinions.* Be prepared to discuss and defend your assumptions and opinions.
7. *Review of the Scene.* Review the scene if necessary. If your testimony is based on an inspection of an accident or crime scene, you may want to revisist the scene shortly before deposition to refresh your memory.
8. *Review Deposition Procedure.* Refresh your memory as to deposition procedures by reviewing this chapter and talking it over with your (client's) lawyer.
9. *Review Expected Questions and Crucial Areas of Testimony.* Your lawyer should advise and prepare you in these areas.
10. *Understand the Legal Issues in the Case.* If you understand the theory of the case, have done your homework, and feel comfortable with your opinions, you should have a satisfactory deposition experience.

DO'S AND DON'TS AT DEPOSITION

By this point, it should be evident that the arduous process of deposition preparation and performance is a crucial aspect of your engagement as an expert witness. Although your own knowledge and resourcefulness are essential factors in your success, the following list of do's and don'ts will provide you with some helpful guidance in dealing with the deposition interrogation.

1. *Do Tell the Truth.* To do otherwise is to invite disaster. You are a hired witness, and you do not have a vested interest in the lawsuit. There should not be any question that you are a professional and are simply calling the shots as you see them. Do not be a "hired gun" whose testimony can be bought. If your testimony cannot be true to your opinions, you should not be in the case (or perhaps you should have been on the other side).
2. *Do Be Professional.* Lawsuits are a serious matter, and presumably you are being well paid for your time. This is no time to clown around or make smart remarks. Your reputation will precede you and will undoubtedly have an effect on future business. Remember that often the deposition may be as far as you get if the case settles. Use your deposition experiences to show your professionalism and enhance your reputation.
3. *Do Not Get Emotional.* If you are a professional and act professionally, you should control emotion. If you allow yourself to become angry or worked up you may be stepping into the lawyers' trap. Stay cool, reserved, and steady. Attempt at all times to respond to questioning in a reserved, thorough, and forthright manner.

> ***Practice Tip:*** **Except for video deposition, the jury is not privy to the mood in the deposition room when remarks are made. Your remarks as they appear on paper, and out of context, can sometimes appear more combative, flippant, or unprofessional than they actually were. It is often one of those "you had to be there" situations.**

4. *Do Not Guess or Assume.* Never assume, unless such assumptions are necessary as a basis for your opinions. If you do make assumptions, they must be based on reasonable

probability. Assumptions or guesses are often a natural temptation but can get you into trouble. Remember: the opposing counsel wants you to agree with him/her. If your lawyer is on the ball he will caution you against guessing or assuming.

EXAMPLE 1

Q:	Do you recall how you received a copy of that letter?
A:	I do not. I assume that a . . .
YOUR LAWYER:	Don't assume. You either know or you don't.
A:	I don't recall how I got it.

EXAMPLE 2

Q:	Did you make any suggestions about any additions in the trust?
YOUR LAWYER:	If you recall.
A:	I don't recall making any suggestions about changes to it.

5. *Do Not Speculate.* Do not try to figure out what the answer is to something you do not know or should not be expected to know. If you are not a lawyer, you should not be expected to express opinions relative to legal matters involved in the case. Generally if this starts to happen, your lawyer will voice an objection.

EXAMPLE

Q:	Under what circumstances would a warranty of the type that appears on the second page of Exhibit 6 be voided?
YOUR LAWYER:	I'm going to object to the form of the question to the extent that it calls on this witness to give an opinion concerning legal conclusions or interpretations of the

> document. To the extent that you can find something in that document which directly responds to the question asked, you may answer, but I'm instructing you not to try to interpret or to speculate on any legal matters.

6. *Do Not Volunteer.* Remember the purposes of a deposition discussed earlier. In a deposition, the other side is trying to get information from you or to discredit your testimony. To volunteer information simply makes their job easier. Save your voluntary comments for the trial (particularly direct examination) when you will attempt to sell your position to the jury. The more information you give the opposition at the deposition level, the better prepared they will be to defuse your trial testimony.
7. *Do Be on the Alert.* This caveat embraces a number of areas reflected by the following examples:

(a) Some questions are too broad to answer.

EXAMPLE

Q: Other than this roofing system, has your company ever constructed a store in which any of those items you were just talking about were not factory mutual approved?

A: That's too broad a question. We've been in business for 75 years.

Caveat: Avoid overbroad questions.

(b) Opposing lawyers frequently tend to make statements and ask you to agree with them.

EXAMPLE

Q: You certainly understood that letter to be a request for coverage, didn't you?

A: I understand it to say what it says. It is an invitation to indemnify, which is what the letter says.

Caveat: Don't let the opposing lawyer put words in your mouth.

(c) Some questions are so convoluted as to be unintelligible and should not be answered without a request for clarification.

EXAMPLE

Q: Do you know if that's something of which Mr. Confucius had knowledge or had communicated to you that he had knowledge about the effect of having work done by someone other than the original subcontractor and its effect on a warranty prior to this memorandum?

A: Well, that's a very difficult question to answer. I don't know how to answer it. You have asked me several different things.

Caveat: Be wary of multipart questions; they are generally confusing. In this case, the question is probably unintelligible, and an even better response would have been a simple "I don't understand the question."

8. *Don't Be Afraid to Admit You Don't Know.* Many times expert witnesses are called to testify in a case because they are also fact witnesses. If you are also testifying as to factual matters, do not hesitate to state that you do not know or do not remember something when that is the case.

EXAMPLE

Q: In 1976, did you prepare a power of attorney for the decedent?

A: I don't remember whether I prepared one in 1976 or not.

9. *Don't Be Intimidated.* Occasionally, the examining attorney will tend to be overconfident, demanding, or sometimes outright obnoxious. Don't let this throw you. Simply continue to answer the questions to the best of your ability, but don't let yourself get boxed into a corner.

EXAMPLE

Q: You did have a lot of communication with General Lee, didn't you?
A: I did.
Q: And he objected to what was going on, didn't he?
A: I don't remember exactly what his objections may have been without reviewing the correspondence.
Q: We will do that later, but you do remember that General Lee was objecting to the manner in which the corporation was being managed back in 1983.
A: I don't remember.
Q: Do you remember that he was complaining about the manner in which money was being borrowed?
A: I don't remember that.
Q: Do you remember that he was objecting because interest was not being paid on money borrowed from the corporation?
A: I'll have to tell you the same thing. Without reviewing the correspondence, I don't remember what he was objecting to.

10. *Do Qualify Your Answer When Necessary.* If you are not sure of a fact, it may be necessary to qualify your answer, for example, "To the best of my recollection." Note in the preceding example how the witness qualified his answer contingent on his review of the correspondence.

EXAMPLE

Q: Do you recall ever seeing this document?
A: I don't recall specifically if we received this one or not.

HOW THE FEDERAL RULES OF PROCEDURE PERTAIN TO DEPOSITIONS

While Rule 26 of the Federal Rules is a provision governing discovery in general, Rules 27 through 32 provide some guidance relative to depositions specifically. A basic knowledge of the highlights and general application of these rules is a useful aid for the expert witness.

Rule 26c—Protective Orders

Rule 26(c) allows any party or the proposed deponent to file a motion seeking relief required to protect a party or person from annoyance, embarrassment, oppression, or undue burden or expense resulting from being deposed. A Motion for Protective Orders requires the applicant to show good cause for the relief requested. Protective Orders can be used to limit the discovery allowed or to prohibit the discovery in its entirety.

> *Practice Tip:* **Rule 26(c) could be relied on by an expert witness in extreme circumstances. However, this rule is not designed for you to use to avoid the taking of your deposition on a date that just happens to be the opening day of deer season or such other minor scheduling conflict.**

Rule 27—Depositions before Action or Pending Appeal

This rule provides some general guidelines that allow the obtaining of depositions to **perpetuate testimony** in matters before an actual lawsuit has been filed.

Rule 28—Persons before Whom Depositions May Be Taken

Rule 28 provides guidelines for the taking of depositions, whether within the United States or in foreign countries, before persons authorized to administer oaths. It also provides that "no deposition shall be taken before a person who is a relative or employee or attorney or counsel of any of the parties, or is a relative or employee of such attorney or counsel, or is financially interested in the action."

Rule 29—Stipulations Regarding Discovery Procedure

As mentioned earlier, this provision enables the parties to make agreements by written stipulations providing the time, place, method, and manner of taking certain depositions; it further allows stipulations modifying the procedural rules applicable at deposition.

Rule 30—Depositions on Oral Examination

The general rule is that, after commencement of the action, any party may take the deposition of any person, including a party, by oral deposition. The party desiring to take a deposition is required to give reasonable written notice to all other parties. (In cases involving several attorneys and key witnesses, deposition scheduling can be a nightmare. You can do your part by being as flexible and reasonable as possible.)

Although it is presumed that most depositions will be taken by stenographic means, the rules do permit a party to file a motion seeking an order approving alternative methods, providing the recorded testimony will be accurate and trustworthy. Telephone depositions are also permitted under this rule. In cases where a public or private business entity is named as the deponent, this rule requires the entity to name one or more officers or other persons to testify and to specify the matters to which they can testify.

As discussed earlier, objections are raised at the deposition but ruled on later by the court.

When the testimony is fully transcribed, the deposition **transcript** must be submitted to the witness for reading, changes, and signature, unless the parties waive signature or the witness is ill, cannot be found, or refuses to sign. Any changes made in the deposition by the witness must be submitted to the deposition officer with reasons for the changes. If the witness does not sign the deposition within 30 days after receiving it, the court reporter signs it and files it with the court. Such depositions are used in the trial of the case as fully and extensively as those that are actually signed by the witness.

The rules provide for the use of copies rather than originals of documents and records after each party has had an opportunity to inspect, copy, and/or verify them.

If a party requesting a deposition fails to show up, this rule makes them liable to the other party for their expenses and attorney's fees incurred in attending. If this should occur during your deposition as an expert witness, your time and expenses should be charged to your party as they would be entitled to reimbursement. In other words, you would not be expected to reduce or dismiss your fee for an appearance just because the deposing party failed to show. Similar rules apply when the witness is not subpoenaed and fails to show, thereby causing unnecessary expenses to one of the other parties.

Rule 31—Depositions on Written Questions

This rule enables any party to take the deposition of any person by propounding written questions. This procedure allows the other party to submit written cross-questions within 30 days of the original questions. The original party has an additional 10 days to submit redirect questions and another 10 days are then allotted to the opposing party for recross questions.

> ***Practice Tip:*** **Written questions are frequently used in medical cases involving several medical care providers where time or expense obviates the practicability of face-to-face oral depositions from each and every care provider.**

Rule 32—Use of Depositions in Court Proceedings

The general rule is that depositions can be used at trial, hearing, or **interlocutory** proceedings, subject to applicable rules of evidence governing admissibility. The deposition can be used against any party having notice of the deposition. If only a part of the deposition is offered into evidence, an adverse party is entitled to introduce any other part of the deposition.

KEY WORDS AND PHRASES

Credibility worthiness of belief; that quality in a witness which renders his evidence worthy of belief.

Entrapment To catch or involve the witness in contradictions.

Interlocutory Provisional; temporary, not final; something intervening which decides some point or matter but is not a final decision of the whole controversy.

Misrepresentation Any manifestation by words or other conduct that amounts to an assertion not in accordance with the facts.

Objection Interposing a declaration to the effect that a particular matter is considered improper or illegal, and submitting the question of its propriety to the court's consideration.

Perpetuating testimony A means or procedure permitted by federal and state discovery rules for preserving for future use the testimony of witnesses, which might otherwise be lost or unavailable before the trial in which it is intended to be used. Fed.R. Civil P. 27(a) (depositions before trial).

Stipulations A binding agreement between counsel respecting various court matters.

Subpoena A process to cause a witness to appear and give testimony.

Subpoena Duces Tecum A process by which the court commands a witness to produce documents or papers in his/her control for trial or deposition.

Sworn testimony Testimony obtained from a witness who has been administered an oath to tell the truth.

Transcript A copy of any kind, though commonly the term refers to a copy of the record of a trial, hearing or other proceeding as prepared by a court reporter.

CHAPTER 6

Direct Examination

The direct examination at trial is a presentation of much of the preparation and testimony provided at the deposition level of the case. Consequently, many of the caveats in Chapter 5 relative to depositions are applicable to the delivery of your testimony in the actual trial. However, due to the greater likelihood of objections by opposing counsel, the presence of the jury and courtroom personnel, and the overall aura of drama relating to the trial proceeding, the direct examination and subsequent cross examination certainly poses a greater challenge than the average deposition.

The presentation of the direct testimony encompasses several areas commencing with the identifying of the expert witnesses; proceeding through a discussion of their backgrounds and qualifications, and the fees and expenses paid to them; and ultimately focusing on the opinion testimony.

In many ways, the direct examination is the most difficult part of your job as an expert witness. The direct examination permits you to draw together all your knowledge, expertise, and preparation so that you can inform the jury in a clear, logical, and convincing manner of your opinions supporting and justifying your client's position. If you are unable to accomplish this, you are not fulfilling your function.

The purpose of presenting an expert witness is to provide the jury with information that can persuade them in the direction of your client. The direct examination is the sole opportunity you will have to accomplish this goal. As will be discussed in Chapter 7, the direct examination will be promptly followed by cross-examination, which has the sole objective of discrediting or mitigating the effect of your direct testimony. Your direct examination is your opportunity "to stand in the sunshine."

ESTABLISHING THE EXPERT'S QUALIFICATIONS

Once the expert witness takes the stand to provide testimony, the first major item of business is to establish his/her credentials and qualifications. Until this has been accomplished, the witness is not properly qualified and will be unable to render opinions of expertise. Although the establishment of proper credentials is often a formality, occasionally the witness does not have sufficient qualifications to serve as an expert. This may be revealed as a result of a challenge by opposing counsel requiring the judge to make a ruling. To overcome this hurdle, the party offering the witness must establish that the witness has the requisite learning, experience, or knowledge to provide opinion testimony. As discussed in Chapter 2, Rule 702 of the Federal Rules of Evidence sets the standard for federal cases; a similar, if not identical, standard has been adopted in most states. The bottom line is that the expert witness must have experience, education, or training that makes the individual more knowledgeable on the subject at hand than the ordinary person. The decision is at the discretion of the judge.

Three Approaches to Establishing Qualifications

Although the establishment of credentials is a necessary formality, it does have a practical side. If a witness has impressive qualifications, the attorney offering the witness will want to get as much "bang for the buck" as possible with the jury. This is particularly true in cases where the verdict could turn on the basis of expert testimony. In such an instance, the attorney will want to demonstrate that his/her expert witness is more credentialed than the opponent's witness (and, therefore, better).

However, the more practical aspect of introducing the expert's qualifications to the jury is deciding how to do it in the most interesting and effective manner. There are three basic methods that can be used.

Detailed Question-and-Answer Method. The first and most straightforward approach is to use detailed questions and answers to provide the information. The following questions illustrate the general framework used by many attorneys. The list is not exhaustive nor will it apply to every situation.

1. State your name for the record, please.
2. Where do you live?
3. What is your occupation?
4. How long have you been so employed?
5. Who is your employer?
6. Please give us a summary of your formal education consisting of dates, schools, areas of study, and so forth.
7. Does that cover all the formal degrees that you have obtained?
8. Have you engaged in any other special studies or courses?
9. Where did those studies take place?
10. Did you receive any special certifications of competence for those studies?

11. Please explain what that certificate means and what is required to attain it.
12. What additional continuing education do you perform each year?
13. What licenses do you hold?
14. Have you done any writing in your field of expertise that has been published?
15. Are you working on any publication at the present time?
16. Please apprise the jury of the speeches and seminars you have presented on this subject.
17. Have you taught any courses?
18. What professional societies and organizations are you a member of?
19. Have you been an officer in any of these organizations?
20. What offices have you held?
21. Have you ever previously testified in a court of law on this type of matter?
22. How many times?

This "traditional method" is generally the most accepted approach and probably the safest from the standpoint of escaping a challenge as to the qualifications of the witness. The problem is that it can become tedious and boring. Obviously, if the jury is lulled to sleep during this testimony, they are going to miss the importance of key credentials. An additional problem with this approach is that some expert witnesses tend to be caught up in their

> ***Practice Tip:*** **Resist the temptation to ramble on about your qualifications. Prepare yourself to present all the salient information in a direct, insightful, and interesting manner.**

own self-worth and engage in an extensive monologue relating everything they have done and accomplished. Obviously, this can be a turnoff to the jury.

The Overview and Fill-in-the-Gap Method. In the second approach, the lawyer will ask you just enough questions to give the jury the flavor of your expertise, while hoping it will be enough to satisfy the judge and opposing counsel as to your qualifications. The rest of the information can be elicited from you throughout your testimony. In this manner, the qualification testimony is less tedious. An additional advantage with this method is the impact that the attorney can create with the jury by interjecting one of your qualifications to support an opinion or observation.

EXAMPLE

Q: Now, Mr. Witness, you have just testified that in your opinion the machine guard was improperly placed and designed.

A: That's correct.

Q: What evidence do you have of your expertise in the designing and placing of machine guards in equipment of this type?

This type of questioning opens the door for you to describe actual studies you have conducted, research you have performed, technical papers you have delivered, or such other information you have acquired that will impact on the **credibility** of your opinion. Obviously, it will be incumbent on your lawyer to ask such a question only where applicable.

For the lawyer, a potential drawback to this approach is that failure to elicit sufficient credentials at the outset may prompt an attack as to whether you are qualified to testify.

Read-the-Resume Method. With the third approach, your credentials are detailed at the outset as in the first method. However, rather than eliciting this information by tedious questioning of the witness, the lawyer simply reads your curriculum vitae and then inquires of you in the following manner:

> Q: Mr. Witness, is that a correct characterization of your background and credentials to testify in this matter?

Utilization of this method still possesses some of the boredom inherent in a detailing of qualifications. Some lawyers attempt to combat this by reading the resume in sections and then asking follow-up questions to break it up a bit.

> EXAMPLE
>
> Q: (After reading your educational background) Does that accurately depict your education and training?
>
> A: Yes, it does.
>
> Q: Now, let's proceed to discuss your work experience for the jury. (Reads that portion of the resume.)

Stipulations as to Qualifications

Occasionally, an opportunity arises when the opposing attorney may stipulate to your qualifications. Again, this is a result of saber rattling between the lawyers. The opposing counsel raises the point, professing that he is "trying to save the court's time" by acceding, without elaboration, to your credentials. In reality, he may feel that your credentials are so compelling that they would be highly persuasive to the jury. Your lawyer, on the other hand, wants the jury to hear the credentials and responds with something along the following lines: "We are certainly prepared to stipulate that Mr. Clever is the most knowledgeable and eminently qualified expert on this subject in the country." Naturally, the opponents are not likely to be interested in such a stipulation, which should open the door to at least an opportunity to cover the most salient aspects of the expert's impressive credentials. On the other hand, if for some reason the expert's qualifications are weak or are likely to cause any bad impressions with the jury, the lawyer offering the witness will be more inclined to accept a stipulation.

The Hired Gun Attack

Occasionally, opposing counsel attacks the credentials of a witness alleging that the individual is merely a hired gun. This theory surfaces in instances where the expert witness has a history and reputation of primarily testifying for the plaintiff, or defendant, as the case may be. The expert's testimony will be "tainted" if the opposing counsel can convince the jury that the expert makes a living going around the country testifying solely for defendants, or plaintiffs. To counter this attack, the offering lawyers need to be able to demonstrate through the witness that substantial work has been performed on both sides of the docket. Even though the witness may have testified exclusively on one side or the other, there may have been instances of nonpartisan consultation or other assistance by the witness. Actually, this can be a two-edged sword if it can be demonstrated that the witness was consulted by the other side but was not asked to testify. The clear implication to the jury is that the testimony would have been unfavorable for the other side.

THE OPINION TESTIMONY

After the expert has been appropriately tendered to the court, the attorney will then proceed to ask questions relative to the opinions of the witness and each and every basis for those opinions. This is characterized as the "opinion testimony." Although the exact questions will vary depending on the case, the law of the jurisdiction, and the attorney's style, the opinion testimony generally will be structured like the following questions:

- *Were you retained to examine the accident scene in this case and to render certain opinions thereon? Or, Have you had occasion to examine and treat the plaintiff in this case?*

As you can see, this question will vary depending on the nature of your involvement.

- *Based on your background, experiences, and your examination and investigation in this case, do you have an opinion based on reasonable scientific probability as to whether . . . ?*

If you are a medical practitioner, the question will be based on "reasonable medical probability" or "reasonable medical certainty" depending on the jurisdiction involved. These magic words must in some way be used to qualify the medical expert's opinion testimony. The language provides some assurance to the court that the opinions are based on generally accepted standards rather than just self-serving "hip shots."

At this point, you are simply being asked whether or not you have an opinion, not what that opinion is. In response, all that is called for is a "yes" or "no" answer (actually, just a "yes" answer unless you're in a hurry to go home!).

- *What is that opinion?*

This question permits you to give a general statement as to your opinion. If you have several opinions, your attorney will probably want you to cover them one at a time.

- *Please tell the jury each and every basis supporting that opinion.*

This is your opportunity to cut loose, depending on the preferences of your attorney. Some attorneys want you to go into detail as to what you have done, what you have observed, and the reason for your opinions. The method of accomplishing this should be prepared in advance between you and your client's counsel.

Other attorneys, however, may wish to maintain more control of the dialogue. If this is the case, the examination in this area will contain a series of subsections.

EXAMPLES

Q: What did you do to arrive at this conclusion?

Q: Why did you run that test?

Q: How did you conduct the test?
Q: How was the analysis done?
Q: What were the results of that test?

During the opinion testimony, your lawyer will want to elicit responses and opinions as to the **proximate cause** or **producing cause** in applicable cases. For example, if you have rendered an opinion that a particular product was defective, testimony will also be required to establish that the defective product was the **producing cause** of the resultant injuries. In other words, the lawyer's burden of proof extends beyond mere occurrence and requires a foreseeable relationship between the resultant injuries and the accident or occurrence.

The Federal Rules of Evidence discussed in Chapter 2 provide the guidelines for determining the data on which experts can rely in formulating their opinions. Rule 703, Federal Rules of Evidence, permits broad latitude to experts in the formulation of their opinions.

Part of the questioning in your opinion testimony may be devoted to defusing the potential effect of cross-examination. The attorney accomplishes this by asking you questions and obtaining responses relative to weak points in your case.

EXAMPLES

Q: In arriving at your opinion, did you take into consideration the plaintiff's age?
Q: Did you also consider that the plaintiff had been involved in prior accidents?
Q: Are you also familiar with the opinions expressed by Dr. Doom, who will be presented by the defense in this case?
Q: Does the opinion of Dr. Doom cause you to change any of your conclusions?

The effect of the foregoing type of question is to target in on the likely focus of attack by the opponent and neutralize the impact of the cross-examination.

DIRECT EXAMINATION TECHNIQUES AND REQUIREMENTS

To properly accomplish the direct examination, the attorney must utilize various techniques. Laying a proper foundation to support testimony, utilizing hypothetical questions, and introducing appropriate exhibits are all useful ways to facilitate direct examination.

Laying Foundations

The Rules of Evidence will generally require that a proper foundation be demonstrated to support the testimony as to certain facts, tests, circumstances, or other matters, before the testimony or physical evidence will be permitted. The purpose of establishing foundations is to satisfy the court that the evidence is reasonably calculated to be fair, reasonable, and credible. For example, before the results of a test are admitted, it is necessary to lay a foundation showing the accuracy of the test and its materiality to the case at hand by asking foundation questions demonstrating these facts. Obviously, the conduct of a test that doesn't assume the same facts and considerations as those fitting the case at hand would be misleading and prejudicial to a jury.

Questions pertaining to the introduction of documents or records are another kind of foundation question. For example, most jurisdictions require the following types of question, based on Rule 803(6) of the Federal Rules of Evidence, to precede the introduction of business records into evidence:

Q: Do these documents constitute a record of the acts, events, conditions, opinions, or diagnoses relative to the injuries sustained by Mr. Jones in his automobile accident of October 1, 1991?

A: Yes.

Q: Were the records made at or near the time of the events they depict?

A: Yes, they were.

Q: And were these records or the entries thereon derived from information transmitted by a person with knowledge?

A: Yes, ma'am.

Q: Were the records kept in the course of your regularly conducted business activities?

A: That's right.

Q: Is it the regular practice in your office procedures to make these records?

A: Yes.

Q: Are you the person who has custody, control, and responsibility for the safekeeping of these records?

A: I am.

Q: And to the best of your knowledge, are these records accurate and trustworthy?

A: Yes, they are.

Hypothetical Questions

Historically, hypothetical questions were necessary to obtain opinion testimony in instances where the expert witness did not have personal knowledge of the facts in the case. Thus, the pertinent facts were incorporated into the hypothetical question propounded to the witness for an opinion. This is, however, a somewhat convoluted technique fostered only to circumvent our own self-imposed rules of evidence.

Consequently, a recent trend has emerged broadening the scope of data on which experts can base their opinions without necessarily resorting to a hypothetical question. Nonetheless, hypothetical questions continue to be commonly utilized, either because they are still required in many jurisdictions, or because the attorney prefers this trial technique in direct examination.

The hypothetical question is based on facts of the case that are either in evidence or that, during the course of the trial, will be admitted into evidence. Accordingly, the hypothetical question requires a thorough recitation of all the applicable facts in the case as a prelude to the opinion. These facts must be a fair representation of the admitted or to-be-admitted evidence. The hypothetical question will be subject to attack unless there is sufficient evidence to support the assumptions on which it is based.

> ***Practice Tip:*** **Because of the complexity of this type of question, it is presumed, and certainly recommended, that your lawyer will thoroughly prepare you in advance of trial for the hypothetical question.**

Most experienced trial lawyers prepare the proposed question in advance and provide the witness, the judge, and opposing counsel with copies to utilize as the question is propounded at trial. With proper preparation and presentation by counsel, the hypothetical question need not be burdensome to the expert witness.

To prepare the jury and the witness for the question, the examiner will generally use some introductory language followed by a recitation of the facts and a request for an opinion. The scenario might be something along the following lines:

THE INTRODUCTION

Q: Doctor, I'm going to ask you a rather lengthy question that asks you to assume the existence of certain facts as a basis for your expert opinion. Is that agreeable?

A: Yes, sir.

THE FACTS

Q: Doctor, I'm going to ask you to assume that . . .

THE HYPOTHETICAL QUESTION

Q: Now Doctor, based on all the foregoing facts, and assuming that all those facts were in evidence in this case, and further based on your qualifications as previously detailed to the jury, do you have an opinion based on a reasonable degree of medical probability as to whether . . . ?

A: Yes.

Q: What is that opinion?

Observe that the hypothetical question may encompass the following three factors: (1) an assumption of the recited facts, (2) an opinion based on previously detailed qualifications of expert, and (3) an opinion based on reasonable probability of practitioners within the field.

The Use and Introduction of Exhibits

We are all familiar with the long-quoted adage, "A picture is worth a thousand words." The use of varied **exhibits** at trial has a comparable effect. They provide something that jurors can see and feel and as a result, the exhibits dramatically embellish the oral testimony in the case. When you are testifying as an expert witness, it is most probable that the direct examiner will have occasion to introduce exhibits through your testimony. The exhibits may be a defective part or product, photographs, charts, diagrams, business records, or similar items.

To introduce such items into evidence, the applicable Rules of Evidence and Procedure require the attorney to meet certain criteria. First, the item or items must be identified by the witness, and second, a proper predicate or foundation for the credibility of the evidence must be established (the witness must vouch for its accuracy). The questions used earlier to lay a foundation for introduction of business records are an example.

In addition to the questions that you answer, the following action will take place in the offering of exhibits into evidence:

1. The exhibit will be offered to the court reporter to be marked with an exhibit number before it is offered to you for identification.

2. After you have identified the exhibit and answered the appropriate questions predicate to its admission for evidence, it will be tendered to opposing counsel for inspection.
3. Next, the exhibit will be handed to the judge with a request that it be admitted to evidence.

EXAMPLE

YOUR COUNSEL:	Your honor, we now offer Plaintiff's Exhibit No. 5 and ask that same be admitted to evidence.
OPPOSING COUNSEL:	No objections, your honor.
JUDGE:	The exhibit is admitted.

4. After the exhibit is admitted, the lawyer will frequently pass the exhibit to the jury for review or may need to retain it for further discussion with the witness.

COMMONLY ENCOUNTERED OBJECTIONS

During your examination as a witness, you can expect to hear various objections voiced for ruling by the court. The lawyers are doing their job by protecting the appellate record and, in many instances, attempting to keep out evidence that is damaging or perhaps not credible. In other words, objections are designed to keep out or limit evidence that is not admissible under the applicable Rules of Evidence and Procedure. To be admissible, the evidence must meet three criteria.

1. It must be material (relate to the issues of the case).
2. It must be relevant (tend to prove or disprove some fact in the case).
3. It must be competent (evidence that is credible, accurate, and not prohibited by specific rules of evidence).

Therefore, objections may be raised to bar evidence that fails to meet these criteria. Although legal scholars tend to vary in their classification or categorization of objection, for the sake of simplicity and brevity, we can generally divide objections into two categories:

1. Objections as to the form of the question.
2. Objections as to the substance of the evidence.

Objections as to Form

These objections relate to the manner in which the question is asked. Without attempting to be all-inclusive, the following examples illustrate such objections:

- *Leading.* This is the most common and well-known objection as to the form of the question. Questions suggesting the answer desired are subject to this objection.

  EXAMPLE

  Q: Were you speeding (as opposed to "How fast were you driving?")?

  Questions that can simply be answered "yes" or "no" are often leading questions.

> ***Practice Tip:*** **The rules in most jurisdictions do allow the use of leading questions in a variety of circumstances such as qualifying expert witnesses, preliminary questions, and so forth.**

- *Asked and Answered.* This objection arises when the examiner keeps asking repetitive questions. On direct examination repetitive questions attempting to embellish a favorable response are likely to draw this objection.

- *Nonresponsive.* A proper objection may be made if the witness answers a question in a manner that is not responsive to the question asked.

  EXAMPLE

Q:	Do you know the manner in which the investigation was conducted?
A:	There wasn't really much investigation needed since it was clear the other driver was at fault.
ATTORNEY:	Objection, the answer is nonresponsive, and we ask that it be stricken from the record and the jury instructed to disregard it.

This objection is raised by the attorney asking the question, not opposing counsel.

- *Narrative.* This objection is frequently used in the testimony of expert witnesses. The opposing counsel may raise this objection when your testimony becomes a narration rather than direct responses to direct questions.

> ***Practice Tip:*** **If the testimony is going well, your attorney will encourage narration, but opposing counsel will strive to limit the testimony to a question-and-answer form.**

Objections as to Substance

This broad category pertains to questions eliciting evidence that may not be admissible. The following illustrations are examples of some of the more prominent objections as to substance.

- *Hearsay.* As a general rule, witnesses are not allowed to testify as to conversations with others outside the presence of the other party. This is a complex area of the law containing many exceptions to the general rule. Chapter 8 provides a more detailed discussion of the Federal Rules of Evidence pertaining to hearsay.

Hearsay is frequently raised as an objection to keep out evidence when the other party has had no opportunity to cross-examine the person making the hearsay statement.

EXAMPLE

Q:	Did you discuss this with the machine operator?
A:	Yes.
Q:	What did he tell you?
OPPOSING COUNSEL:	Objection, that's hearsay.

- *Irrelevant.* This is a general objection opposing a question that calls for a response that is clearly irrelevant to the lawsuit.
- *Immaterial.* This is another general objection and opposes questions calculated to obtain information that is not material to the issues in the case. The case issues are formulated by the pleadings of the parties. The variance in the affirmative and responsive pleadings in the case form the disagreements constituting the issues.

EXAMPLE

Q:	Did the other driver appear to have been drinking?
OPPOSING COUNSEL:	We object, your honor. This is not an issue and is immaterial. We have admitted liability, and there are no pleadings for **punitive damages**.

- *Best Evidence Rule.* The **best evidence rule** applies only to testimony based on documentary evidence. The basis of the objection is that the document itself provides the best and most credible evidence; therefore, the explanatory testimony of the witness should be prohibited.
- *Failure to Lay a Proper Foundation.* This complaint encompasses a variety of objections such as efforts by witnesses to testify on matters for which they have not been shown to be qualified, failure to establish a foundation for introduction of exhibits, and so forth. The following illustration reflects the type of questions that must be asked and answered to establish a proper predicate for the admissibility of the contents of a discussion with the plaintiff and the defendant:

EXAMPLES

Q: Did you have an occasion to have a meeting on this subject where the plaintiff and defendant were both present?

Q: Where did this meeting take place?

Q: Who else was present?

Q: What time of day did this take place?

Q: Please tell us what the parties said.

In summary, a wide variety of objections can be raised in trial on either direct or cross-examination. Chapter 7, will focus further attention on objections that are frequently encountered during cross-examination.

However, whether engaged in direct or cross-examination, a witness can expect objections to be interjected. To function at maximum capacity, the expert witness should have a good basic understanding of the different types of objections that may arise as well as their purpose. If properly prepared with this background, the expert can perform with greater confidence and effectiveness.

USEFUL RULES IN PREPARING FOR DIRECT EXAMINATION

Even with experience or preparation, testifying as a witness is arduous. Your initial appearance in the trial of the case is the direct examination, and this sets the stage for your entire trial performance. The following rules will help you prepare for this experience so you can testify in a professional and successful manner. If you are already a seasoned witness, use these rules to review and brush up on potential problem areas.

- *Use Down-to-Earth Language.* Don't attempt to impress the jury with five-dollar words. Try to relate to them as an average person and use understandable language. It has already been established that you are the expert so teach the jury in language they can relate to, not technical parlance.
- *Appear Objective and Impartial.* Don't be an advocate. The client already has a lawyer. Your job is to communicate your findings and opinions to the jurors in a convincing and believable manner. If you appear one sided it will taint your testimony.
- *Don't Volunteer.* As in deposition, you should answer all questions clearly and fairly, but do not volunteer extraneous information that can be picked up for cross-examination.
- *Review all Your Prior Publications for Possible Inconsistency with Your Expected Current Testimony.* It is a good idea to maintain copies of all your writings for ready reference. In any event you will probably be asked to produce copies to opposing counsel so you may as well have it handy. Also keep copies of all prior depositions as you can always review what you said in an earlier case.
- *Do Not Comment on the Case Publicly.* It is not your position to discuss the case with television, radio, or newspaper reporters, or other media representatives.

- *Be Prepared to Stand Your Ground.* To a large extent, cross-examination focuses on the weaknesses or "chinks" developed in your direct examination. So prepare to present your testimony clearly and convincingly on direct so you can stand your ground on cross-examination.
- *Look at the Jurors.* When responding to important questions or making key points, look at the jurors and let them see your sincerity. During the course of direct examination you should have eyeballed each juror at least once. Don't devote your attention to only two or three jurors. They must all be convinced.
- *Maintain a Professional Appearance.* Dress and groom professionally. Do not slouch in the witness chair; it makes you appear rebellious and disrespectful. Avoid flashy jewelry and do not chew gum.
- *Maintain a Pleasant Demeanor.* Try to have a pleasant look on your face and appear attentive and interested at all times. Be courteous and respectful to the judge, attorneys, and all others. Avoid fraternizing with the jurors or showing acts of familiarization such as waves, winks, and unwarranted smiles.
- *Be Cautious about Estimating Times, Distances, or Speeds.* Estimates can be used against you on cross-examination.
- *Listen Carefully to All Instructions and Recommendations from Your Counsel.* Your attorney will advise you as to any materials you may or should bring to court and will prepare you for his questions including hypothetical questions. If you follow your attorneys instructions you should be well-prepared for direct examination.
- *Be Attuned to the Burdens of Your Direct Examiner.* Remember that the Rules of Evidence and Procedure limit your examiner from focusing on leading questions, so you need to stay alert and responsive. Also, be attuned to the messages sent by objections and be aware of the purpose and nature of the questions propounded to you by the direct examiner.

REDIRECT EXAMINATION

The final aspect of direct examination is the redirect. Not every case involves redirect examination. However, if the cross examiner has pierced your armor, some redirect may be required to "plug the holes." During redirect you need to be particularly alert and responsive to your attorney, who may be attempting to rehabilitate some of your prior testimony.

KEY WORDS AND PHRASES

Best evidence rule Rule which requires that the best evidence available be presented in lieu of less satisfactory evidence. Therefore, contents of a document must be proved by producing the document itself.

Exhibit A paper or document produced and exhibited to a court during trial in proof of facts that, upon being accepted, is marked for identification and filed of record or otherwise made part of the case.

Form of the question In contradistinction to substance, form means the legal or technical manner to be observed in the framing of questions at trial.

Producing cause An efficient, existing, or contributing cause which, in natural and continuing sequence, produces the injury or damage complained of.

Proximate cause That which, in a natural and continuous sequence, unbroken by any efficient intervening cause, produces injury and without which the result would not have occurred.

Punitive damages Also referred to as exemplary or enhanced damages; those damages awarded to plaintiff over and above actual damages with the purpose of setting an example by the defendants wrongful behavior.

CHAPTER 7

Cross-Examination

The cross-examination is the culmination of all that has transpired from the inception of your involvement in the case. This is your time to "go to the wall." Your veracity and believability are being tested and the results will have a telling impact on the jurors.

Cross-examination is an art, and some lawyers have better techniques than others. Many lawyers believe that cross-examination of the key witnesses makes the difference between winning and losing the case. In any event, you can be assured that the opponent's lawyer will have a plan for your cross-examination and will be well-prepared to implement it.

GOALS OF CROSS-EXAMINATION

Although the specific style and purpose of a cross-examination varies from case to case depending on the various facts and circumstances, cross-examination serves several common objectives or goals. Not all these goals or purposes are applicable to every case, and they will vary at the cross-examiner's discretion. The following sections discuss several possible areas of attack.

Lack of Qualifications

Lack of qualifications presents the initial opportunity for an attack of the expert witness. As discussed in previous chapters, unless the expert has sufficient credentials to meet the qualification standard, the testimony will not be admitted. In some cases, the expert may qualify in general terms but fail to qualify relative to crucial issues involved in the case. An attack in this area usually involves questions as to prior training, education, or experience.

EXAMPLE

Q: Doctor since your graduation from medical school 25 years ago, you haven't had any further training in orthopedic surgery, have you?

A: No.

Q: And isn't it also true that you haven't completed any specialized courses in the field of orthopedic surgery?

A: No, I have not.

Q: And you aren't a fellow of the American Academy of Orthopedic Surgery or any other specialist group of that type.

A: That's true, I'm not.

Discrediting the Witness

This approach focuses on diminishing or destroying the impact of the witness's testimony on direct examination. One way to do this is to attack the integrity of the witness. Is the witness obviously lying? Has he/she been previously convicted of a major crime? Is the witness a hired gun? All these areas offer the cross-examiner opportunities to assail and discredit the witness.

The exact methods or questioning used by the cross-examiner will vary, but if there is a potentially damaging area the cross-examiner will ferret it out, exploit it, and strive to do as much damage as possible.

> ***Practice Tip:*** **Not all criminal convictions are fair game to the cross-examiner. Minor charges and convictions far in the past are exempt. If you have anything on your record, you should discuss it with your attorney in advance so you can be properly advised and protected.**

Focusing on Illogical or Improbable Conclusions and Opinions

With this technique, the cross-examiner attempts to illustrate that the preparation, analysis, or methodology utilized by the expert is impractical or incorrect in one or more respects, or, possibly, that it is downright absurd. Occasionally, the information relied on by the expert in reaching his or her conclusions is based on inaccurate or incomplete information. In this scenario, the examiner will require a detailing of the facts and information relied on, how the opinions were formed, and the reliability of the equipment and technology utilized. Once a weak point is exposed, the questioning will zero in accordingly.

> ***Practice Tip:*** **Your expert's report, deposition, testimony in other cases, or learned treatises may all be utilized by the cross-examiner in an attempt to expose faulty reasoning or methodology.**

Showing Bias or Prejudice

The cross-examiner will be looking for indications of favoritism or bias. Consider the following possibilities.

1. Do you nearly always testify for the plaintiff? or the defense?
2. Are you being paid an inordinately high fee for the work being performed in the case?
3. Do you have a history of testifying for this same client? Or their law firm?
4. Do you have a social relationship with your client or members of their law firm?
5. Have you ever been employed by the client? or their law firm?
6. Do you have any type of interest in the outcome of the lawsuit that would benefit you?

The opposing counsel will also be looking for indications that the expert has a prejudicial outlook as to the outcome of the case or the subject matter. For example, assume a case involving a suit on a fire insurance policy against an insurance company. Assume further that the insurer defends by alleging that the insured is an arsonist. If the insurance company presents a witness who makes a living investigating arsons, it may be possible to show that the witness has a biased or unreasonably cynical outlook that taints his/her perceptions and testimony.

Impeachment

It seems that all cross-examiners are constantly seeking **impeachment** opportunities. The sole objective of impeachment is to impair the credibility of the witness with the jury. One effective way of accomplishing this is either to expose contradictory statements by the witness during the trial testimony, or to show contrary statements in prior testimony, that is, deposition. Impeachment also can arise as a result of inconsistencies between oral testimony and documentary evidence. For example, a discrepancy between what you say in your report and the statements you make at trial can set you up for impeachment.

The focus in impeachment is not on the truth or accuracy of evidence, but rather on inconsistencies that raise issues as to the reliability or believability of the witness. In other words, impeachment proof is not **substantive evidence,** but merely serves to undermine the credibility of the witness. Inconsistent statements, contradictions, hostility, bias, and lack of capacity all can be utilized for impeachment purposes.

> *Practice Tip:* **Impeachment is limited to material issues, and the court should not allow a cross-examiner to split hairs over inconsequential matters simply in an effort to impeach the testimony of an expert witness.**

EXAMPLE

Q: Do you recall making that statement in your deposition?
A: No.
Q: Would you disagree now with that statement?
A: No.

The questioning here is simply fishing for a misstatement without any real basis for complaint in an effort to manufacture impeachment.

Impeachment does not depend on the degree of inconsistency when statements are in variance. The inconsistency per se is simply available to the jury for their consideration as to its impact on the believability of the witness.

Obtaining Admissions and Concessions

This is considered to be a very effective accomplishment in cross-examination of experts. In some instances, the sole objective of cross-examination may be to get a simple **admission** or concession or two from an expert witness who is otherwise very convincing in his/her opinion testimony.

EXAMPLE

Q: You have testified that there was no deviation from the ordinance in the installation of this equipment, is that right?

A: Correct.

Q: But, the ordinance also applies to the operation of this equipment, does it not?

A: Yes, it does.

Q: And the last paragraph, there, of the ordinance is very specific regarding the operating requirements, is it not?

A: That's true.

Q: Those requirements were not fully followed in this case, were they?

A: Not entirely.

The cross-examiner could stop at this point, having this concession, or could proceed to seek further concessions. In this case, the cross-examiner avoided a confrontation with the expert who voiced strong opinions relative to the proper installation of the equipment and instead obtained a concession relative to the operation of the equipment.

> ***Practice Tip:*** **As an expert witness, you may never know what the cross-examiner is up to, but the more you know about their methods and goals, the less likely you are to get into serious trouble.**

PREPARING FOR CROSS-EXAMINATION

Now that you have a taste of cross-examination and its goals and purposes, your next logical concern is likely to be: What can I do to prepare for it?

Knowing What to Prepare For

Obviously, to prepare for anything successfully, you need to know what you are preparing for. In this sense, it may help to be aware of techniques that are taught to trial lawyers who are seeking to develop or perfect cross-examination skills. Perhaps one of the best and most succinct summaries of cross-examination techniques was developed by law professor Irving Younger, who formulated the "Ten Commandments of Cross-Examination." You can improve your skills as an expert witness by learning how these commandments can help the cross-examiner and how they can be applicable to you.

The Ten Commandments of Cross-Examination

1. *Be Brief.* Younger advises lawyers that the less time they spend standing up talking, the less frequently they will screw up. That's probably good advice for anybody.
2. *Use Plain Words.* This requires little explanation and is a caveat that may be even more important to the expert witness than to the cross-examiner. Obviously, if you don't talk in plain language, the jurors will not understand you; and if they don't understand you, you cannot effectively impress them with your opinions.
3. *Use Only Leading Questions.* The point here is that cross-examiners are trained to maintain control of the trial dialogue, set the course, and use **leading questions** all the way. The best you can do is stay on the alert, look for your openings, and use them wisely. Fortunately, even the best of

cross-examiners sometimes fail to adhere to this caveat and may occasionally ask questions that allow you to maneuver beyond "yes or no" responses. Be on the alert for these opportunities.

4. *Be Prepared.* The basic idea is that the cross-examiner should know what the witness is going to say, know what areas to exploit, and should never ask questions if they don't know what the answer will be. You will be able to determine very quickly whether your cross-examiner is well prepared. You should govern yourself accordingly.
5. *Listen.* Younger cautions lawyers to listen to the responses they receive rather than get so wrapped up in what question they are going to ask next that they miss a golden opportunity. Expert witnesses can benefit from this advice by listening closely to the exact wording of the questions and being certain that their responses are appropriate.
6. *Do Not Quarrel.* This is good advice for expert witnesses as well as lawyers. Your client has hired you to help develop the war plans, not to fly the fighter jet.
7. *Avoid Repetition.* This commandment cautions lawyers not to rehash questions asked on direct examination or to give witnesses an opportunity to repeat what they have already said since it provides the witness another opportunity to tell his/her story to the jury.
8. *Disallow Witness Explanation.* On the other hand, explanation may be essential to an understanding of your position. If an explanation is needed, offer it and put the burden back on the cross-examiner. Ultimately, it is up to the judge to decide when explanation is allowed.
9. *Limit Questioning.* The idea here is that if a point or concession has been scored, the cross-examiner should stop while ahead rather than asking additional questions that may result in explanations or responses negating the impact previously achieved. However, if the lawyer is not savvy enough

to realize when he/she has clipped one of your wings, you may get an opportunity to repair the damage.

10. *Save for Summation.* This is similar to Commandment 9. Younger suggests that in some situations the cross-examiner can save the ultimate point for jury argument.

Doing Your Homework

When it comes to being prepared for cross-examination, there is no replacement for doing your "homework." To be properly prepared you should do all of the following:

1. *Review Pleadings and Depositions.* In essence, you need to freshen your memory on the materials you relied on in reaching your opinions and conclusions in the case.

2. *Review Your Deposition.* You should thoroughly reread your deposition, your opinion report, and any other statements you have made. In reading your deposition, look for potential weak areas, or those areas where the cross-examiner is likely to focus, and prepare for them. Be fully prepared on your past statements so you can avoid inconsistencies that would lead to impeachment. If there are any changes, be prepared to explain them.

3. *Review Exhibits.* Review all insurance policies, contracts, memoranda, and other documents that will be likely exhibits in the case, and make sure you are thoroughly familiar with them.

4. *Create a Potential Question-and-Answer List.* Your attorney should work with you on this. Once the pattern of direct examination is established, you should work on anticipating potential cross-examination questions and your answers.

5. *Be Prepared on the Details.* All your preparation is likely to be based on a multitude of factual details and information. To effectively respond and hold your own on cross-examination, you must have a thorough remembrance and understanding of all the details.

6. *Review Past Publications.* If you have previously written in the subject area or have given testimony on similar matters in other cases, it is very important to refresh your memory on these points to circumvent attempts by the cross-examiner to set you up for impeachment or harmful admissions.

SOME RULES AND GUIDELINES FOR CROSS-EXAMINATIONS

Many of the suggestions and items of advice discussed in Chapters 5 and 6 are equally valuable in preparing for cross-examination. In addition, the following areas require particular attention, as described, when coping with cross-examination:

1. *The Cross-Examination Theme.* As previously discussed, experienced cross-examiners will have formulated their objectives or theme of attack before they commence the questioning. Although it's always a risk to assume anything, you may be a bit ahead of the game if you can detect the thrust of the questioning as it transpires. Be alert for the following possibilities:

- **a.** Questions regarding statements on direct examination obviously intended to attack or diminish the significance of what was stated.
- **b.** Examination relative to matters showing bias or prejudice.
- **c.** Impeachment attempts based on prior inconsistent statements in the case.
- **d.** Impeachment attempts based on statements contained in prior books, articles, or testimony in other cases.
- **e.** Interrogation relative to training experience or background indicating an attempt to discredit your qualification as an expert witness.

f. A long series of questions pertaining to your testing, analysis, conclusions, or opinions, designed to discredit the accuracy of your work or to obtain certain admissions or concessions.

2. *Evasiveness.* An appearance of evasiveness looks bad to the jury. It is important to give an impression of candor and forthrightness. By the same token, you don't want merely to be a "marionette" waiting for the cross-examiner to pull your strings. It is difficult to maintain a middle ground. Nonetheless, there are some things you should not do. Do not attempt to evade by arguing with the attorney. Do not evade by frequently saying "I do not remember" unless there is no other applicable answer. While it is okay not to remember (and you should always be truthful), the constant inability to remember things will ultimately have an adverse effect on the jury.

It generally looks bad to answer a question with a question. This form of evasiveness may imply that you have something to hide. In some circumstances, it appears downright obnoxious or disrespectful.

So, what can you do? The bottom line is that you must be alert, well prepared on the details, and capable of sticking to your position. If a question causes you concern, you can ask counsel to rephrase the question or attempt to rephrase the question yourself.

EXAMPLE

A: Are you asking me if . . . ?

This will at least allow you some time to consider your response. Even this type of response, however, will be perceived as evasive if it is overdone.

3. *Questions by the Judge.* In some jurisdictions or circumstances, the judge may intervene in the cross-examination and ask

some questions of his/her own. However, this is not normally the case and often poses problems for the attorneys as well as the witness. Nevertheless, you should be prepared for such a possibility and not be deterred or misdirected if this occurs. You will be obligated to respond, but you should be guided by the same rules and caveats as if the questions were coming from the cross-examiner. Everything you say is being heard by the jury so you cannot let your guard down.

4. *Form of Questions.* Just as in depositions, or even direct examination, you must be attuned to the question being asked. Be alert for questions that are compounded, multiple part, confusing, or unintelligible. Always wait until a question is complete before attempting to respond to it. If the answer requires an explanation, give your answer and ask the judge to allow you to explain it.

5. *Appearance and Demeanor.* Your appearance and demeanor as a witness are always important. I believe it is especially important during cross-examination. In many cases, the jury perceives the dialogue between the expert witness and the cross-examining attorney as a real "battle of wills," a confrontation of professionals. It is important for you to make as favorable a physical impression as the lawyer. You should be sitting up straight and alert. You should not appear confused, frustrated, or antagonized. You should strive to appear confident and in control of yourself. Remember always that your body language can belie what you speak.

6. *File Materials.* Many a witness has been embarrassed at trial as the cross-examiner seizes their files or notes and uses it to cross-examine them. You should not have anything with you that has not be previously disclosed to and discussed with your attorney. If you do not bring a file or notes with you to court, you should also be prepared for cross-examination on this point, particularly if you had notes but must admit that you threw them away before trial. Remember, the goal of the cross-examiner is to expose the chinks in your armor.

7. *Mind Your Manners.* I always advocate the liberal use of "Yes, Sir [or Ma'am]" and "No, Sir" [or Ma'am] in responding to questions by the attorneys since it connotes formality and a respect for the decorum of the courtroom. Jurors expect this type of respect for the system, and as we have previously discussed, the impression you make with the jury is of paramount importance. When addressing the judge the proper title is Your Honor and address the attorneys by title and last name, for example, Ms. Stern.

8. *Get the Question Straight.* As stated earlier, be certain you understand the question before you attempt to answer it. If the question isn't clear or if you are simply having difficulty getting it straight in your mind, ask the lawyer to restate it.

9. *Speak Plain English.* Remember, communication is the name of the game. The jury must understand you and you must not offend them. So, avoid fancy or technical words, don't use slang or vulgar expressions, and be sure to speak distinctly and loud enough so that all can hear. Face the jury when you are giving important testimony or explanations.

10. *Be Wary of Assumptions.* Occasionally the cross-examiner will ask the witness to assume certain facts and then respond to questions based on those facts. This technique may be used to gain admissions or concessions on important points. Sometimes the cross-examiner may be basing the question on facts that actually exist in the case, of which the expert is unaware. In other instances, the facts may not apply and therefore should, but may not, draw an objection from your client's attorney. When confronted with questions of this sort, you should consider the facts carefully. If they don't fit the situation or are based on an unreasonable premise, do not allow yourself to be boxed in.

EXAMPLE

A: I'm sorry, but you're asking me to express an opinion on facts that don't fit this case, and I cannot give you an opinion on abstract facts out of context.

PLOYS AND GAMES OF THE CROSS-EXAMINER

Once you understand the ground rules of cross-examination, the objectives of the cross-examiner emerge in clear focus. To accomplish their objectives, cross-examiners may utilize any of many techniques. The following examples are but some of the many "ploys" or "games" relied on by the resourceful cross-examiner.

1. *The Yogi Berra Approach.* Yogi has been often quoted for his observation, "it ain't over until it's over." This is certainly true of cross-examination. Occasionally, a cross-examiner will employ this technique after a long and tedious cross-examination and redirect examination by remarking, "I don't have anything else." Then, as you prepare to leave the witness chair, he or she pipes up with, "Oh!, by the way, just one more quick question." The attorney hopes that by this time you have begun to relax or let your guard down just a bit. What then follows is not an innocuous query as you may expect, but, instead, a vital question probably backed up by several additional questions calculated to gain a key concession, admission, or other point when you are least expecting it. This technique also enables the cross-examiner to finish on a strong point. So, remember to keep your "chin covered" until it is truly over.

2. *The Double Negative.* Questions phrased in double negative language can be confusing and tricky, and it is not always clear whether the correct answer is "yes" or "no."

EXAMPLE

Q: You're not telling us you didn't administer the test, are you?

The best way to respond to this type of question is with a straight statement.

EXAMPLE

A: I did not personally administer the test.

3. *Stuffing Words in Your Mouth.* Lawyers are great at using leading questions to suggest the desired response.

EXAMPLE

Q: You didn't actually expect the test to be conclusive, did you?

The lawyer is setting you up for the response desired and is, in effect, "stuffing words in your mouth." Don't fail to form your own opinions and stick by your guns. Don't let the cross-examiner draw you into inaccurate concessions or statements.

4. *The Good Ole Boy.* This is, in effect, a style of cross-examination whereby the lawyer uses countrified charm to disarm the witness and to court the jury. Remember, when you are on the witness stand, you are in an adversarial position and must never . . . never let your guard down.

5. *The Fisherman's Ploy.* Much like a fisherman, the cross-examiner will keep casting the same line by you time and time again until he/she either gets the desired response or one that differs from your other answers to the same question. That response can be used for impeachment or, more likely, in jury argument. The only way to avoid this trap is to stay consistent in your answers to the same or similar questions. If your attorney is on the ball he/she will object that the question has been asked and answered which may get you off the hook.

6. *The Appeal to Vanity.* Witnesses, and expert witnesses in particular, hate to admit that they don't know something. The cross-examiner can use this to advantage by appealing to the vanity of the witness.

EXAMPLE

Q: As Superintendent on the project, didn't you know that the machinery couldn't be used in that manner for an extensive period of time without breakdown or repairs?

This type of question may cause a witness to respond "yes" because they don't want to admit they don't know something. The problem is that the foregoing statement may not be correct to begin with. A satisfactory response may have been:

A: No, as far as I'm concerned the machinery was properly used.

7. *Is There a Question on the Floor?* Some lawyers use rather subtle techniques to elicit information from witnesses without even asking a question. Of course, your only obligation is to answer questions as they are asked, and you should never volunteer anything to the cross-examiner. Make them seek it out.

One example of this technique occurs when the lawyer makes a statement and then waits for you to respond. Remember, if the comment is not in the form of a question, you have no duty to respond.

An even trickier example is the so-called silent treatment. Here the lawyer responds to your answer with silence. He/she continues to look at you as though further response is expected and may further embellish this technique with theatrical techniques such as a raised eyebrow or a quizzical look as if to say, "What else?" or "Go on!" This type of approach often causes some witnesses to feel uncomfortable or compelled to continue. You should not fall for this technique. Your duty to respond exists only when there is a "question on the floor."

8. *The Bottomless Well.* Here the lawyer asks open-ended questions. Unless you respond specifically, your response can be twisted in final argument and have a damaging effect.

EXAMPLE

Q: Was the water deep?

How deep is deep? Is it the proverbial bottomless well? Don't fall into this trap. Your response should be specific.

A: The water was 2 1/2 feet deep in that area.

9. *The Mousetrap Technique.* The purpose of this technique is to set impeachment traps. The cross-examiner asks questions that have been previously addressed in deposition and attempts to catch you in the mousetrap by making an answer conflict with prior responses. If this happens, the lawyer then springs the trap and sets up impeachment by asking the appropriate foundation questions to establish the impeachment and impair your credibility with the jury.

EXAMPLE

Q: You recall appearing in my office on June 9, 1991, and giving your deposition?

A: Yes, I do.

Q: You were sworn in and gave your testimony under oath, didn't you?

A: Yes.

Q: You understood that your testimony given under oath was the same as if you were actually in the courtroom before the judge and jury?

A: Yes, sir.

Q: You were represented by counsel and your attorney was with you at the deposition, correct?

A: That's right.

Q: You were provided the opportunity to read your copy of the deposition and note any corrections, weren't you?

A: Yes, sir.

Q: Do you recall testifying that . . . ?

A: Not in that way.

Q: Let me refer you to page 29, line 14 of your deposition, and follow me as I read the question. (The question is read.)

Q: Did I read that correctly?

A: Yes.

Q: Now, please read to the court and jury the answer you gave under oath at that time.

The trap is now sprung and the cross-examiner is not going to allow you to embellish or explain the answer. If you feel that an explanation is warranted, however, you can request permission of the judge to explain it, which may or may not be granted, at the judge's discretion.

> ***Practice Tip:*** **To avoid getting caught in the mousetrap, you must be thoroughly conversant with your past testimonies and comments and be consistent in your responses.**

10. *The Paid Witness.* In this scenario, the cross-examiner seems to make something out of the fact that you are being paid by the other side.

EXAMPLE

Q: You are being paid to come here today and testify that your client driver wasn't responsible for this accident, aren't you?

The pitfall here is that neither a simple yes or no answer is fully correct. Presumably, you are being compensated as an expert witness, so a no answer would not be correct. Conversely, a yes answer implies that you are being paid not only to be there but for the testimony you are giving. This bomb needs to be defused by a response of the following nature:

A: I am not being paid for my testimony since that is my honest assessment of the facts. However, I am being compensated for my time in appearing here today to give my opinion to the court and jury.

11. *Musical Chairs.* In this scenario, the ploy is confusion. The cross-examiner jumps from one set of circumstances or time

frame to another. Often, this is skillfully done and, unless you stay alert, you may find yourself giving answers that were true in one set of circumstances, but not another. The cure is twofold. First, stay alert and follow the questioning closely. Second, when the music stops and you are expected to answer, don't hesitate to ask for a clarification of the time, place, subject matter, or circumstances, before you grab your chair.

12. *Precisely Speaking.* Although you should always strive to give specific answers, be watchful of attempts by the cross-examiner to obtain answers pinning you down too precisely. Often, this is an invitation to guess at a time, distance, speed, or other circumstance beyond a general approximation. If you don't know, you should say so, and never guess. If you guess wrong, your response may be very harmful to your testimony or the case.

EXAMPLE

Q: How long was the pin?
A: I'm not sure.
Q: Was it longer than 6 inches?
A: No.
Q: Was it less than an inch?
A: No.
Q: Would it be fair to say 3 inches?
A: It was somewhere between 1 inch and 6 inches.

13. *Discussions with the Client's Lawyer.* The implication here is that there is something sordid about having discussed the case with your client's lawyer. The obvious further inference is that the lawyer told you what to say. Many lawyers cut this technique off in advance by bringing it up on direct examination. However, if they fail to do so, the astute examiner will often delve into it on cross-examination. If this happens to you, you should quickly and forthrightly admit that you have had occasion to discuss the case with your client's attorney. This will usually cause

the cross-examiner to move on to another subject. If you are asked whether the lawyer told you what to say or how to testify, your response should be along the following lines.

EXAMPLE

A: He told me to always tell the truth.

14. *The Catch 22 Question.* We have all heard about this classic trick question.

EXAMPLE

Q: Have you stopped beating your wife yet?

With either a yes or a no answer, you are caught between the rock and the hard place. If you must answer this type of question, you have to make a positive statement.

EXAMPLE

A: I have never beat my wife.

15. *The Pointed Finger.* Here the finger is pointed at your client reflecting an aspersion of guilt. This approach is common in product liability situations and may also apply in negligence cases.

EXAMPLE

Q: Honestly, don't you believe that a better design would have made this toy safer for children?

This ploy is designed to obtain a concession or admission that probably the design could have been better. In all probability, hindsight may suggest that something better could have been done. However, the real issue should be whether this specific toy was properly and safely designed, not whether it could possibly be better. You have to face this sort of question head-on.

EXAMPLE

A: I don't know what you mean by better, but I believe this toy was designed in a safe and proper manner.

> ***Practice Tip:* The course of cross-examination is laden with bunkers and other hazards. However, if you stay alert and practice your skills, you can par the course. Good luck!**

KEY WORDS AND PHRASES

Admissions Confessions, concessions, or voluntary acknowledgments made by a party of the existence of certain facts. They are statements against the interest of the party making them.

Conclusive evidence That which is incontrovertible either because the law does not permit it to be contradicted or because it is so strong and convincing as to overbear all proof to the contrary and establish the proposition in question beyond any doubt.

Impeachment The adducing of proof that a witness is unworthy of belief.

Leading question One which instructs the witness how to answer or puts into his mouth words to be echoed back.

Substantive evidence That adduced for the purpose of proving a fact in issue, as opposed to evidence given for the purpose of discrediting a witness.

CHAPTER 8

Some Final Tips and Thoughts

This final chapter draws together and builds on the material in the preceding chapters. To some extent, it also fills in some gaps with valuable information not discussed, or only partially treated, in prior chapters.

At this point, you should have a thorough understanding of the world of the expert witness—the skills required, the rigors of preparation, and methods of dealing with the courtroom challenge. Earlier chapters have also discussed legal terms, fee setting, marketing, and the applicable rules of evidence, and civil procedure. So what is left?

First, this chapter provides some specific information and observations for various fields of expertise. Second, it discusses how some of the unique characteristics of witnesses can interpose with the styles and characteristics of lawyers. Next is a review of the rules of evidence as they pertain to hearsay, and the chapter ends with some commentary in the form of pertinent questions and answers for the expert witness.

SPECIAL CONSIDERATIONS FOR YOUR AREA OF EXPERTISE

Until now our discussion has been broad enough in scope to encompass problems, procedures, and scenarios pertaining to almost any area of expertise. In this section, the focus is on information pertaining to selected specialty areas.

Medical Practitioners

Physicians, surgeons, and other medical practitioners undoubtedly constitute the largest category of expert witness in both civil and criminal trials.

Direct Examination. The following checklist exemplifies the general categories of questioning conducted with medical practitioners in deposition or direct examination.

1. *Identification.* Name, residence, and profession.
2. *Qualifications.* Schooling, degrees, medical societies, publications, teaching experience, specialties, hospital associations, certificates, and awards.
3. *Patient's History.* This is generally permissible hearsay.
4. *Examination.* Both objective and subjective.
5. *Diagnostic Procedures.* X-rays, laboratory work, tests, etc.
6. *Findings*

   EXAMPLES

   Q: What did the examination reveal to you?
   Q: What were the results of each test conducted?

7. *Diagnosis*

   EXAMPLE

   Q: Based on the history, your examination, and testing, what was your diagnosis?

8. *Treatment*

EXAMPLES

Q: Did you have occasion to treat Mrs. Hurt?
Q: What treatment did you recommend or provide?

9. *Causal Relationship*

EXAMPLES

Q: Doctor, based on everything we discussed, do you have an opinion with reasonable medical probability and certainty as to whether the injuries you diagnosed for Mrs. Hurt were caused solely as a result of her auto accident on January 5, 1992?
Q: What is your opinion?

10. *Prognosis.* Requests a statement of your prognosis for the patient relative to state of health, degree of recovery, treatment, and care.

11. *Fee Charges.* You will be requested to testify as to the necessity and reasonableness of your medical charges and possibly those of other medical care providers as well.

12. *Future Medical Care*

EXAMPLES

Q: Will future medical care and treatment be required for Mrs. Hurt due to the injuries she incurred in this auto accident?
Q: What type of care and treatment will be required?
Q: What is your estimate of the costs of this future medical treatment and care?

The following list shows 100 typical questions calculated to elicit the opinion of medical practitioners.

Due to the time, expense and scheduling problems of testifying live in the courtroom the direct testimony of physicians and surgeons is often accomplished by video taped deposition.

Specific Questions for Dr. Treatum

1. Please tell the Judge and jury your name.
2. Doctor, you are licensed to practice medicine in the State of Texas, are you not?
3. In what year did you become licensed as a physician in Texas?
4. How long have you practiced?
5. Where have you practiced?
6. Doctor, we are taking your deposition by agreement between the attorneys and your office so that we won't have to call you to trial when the case is called. You won't be before the jury in person, so I'm going to ask you some preliminary questions so that the jury might have a better understanding about your qualifications and your background as an expert in this case.
7. Please state where you took your undergraduate work, the degree earned, if any, and the year of your graduation.
8. Where did you take your professional training?
9. In what year did you graduate and with what degree?
10. Where did you intern?
11. For what period of time was your internship?
12. What was the nature of that training?
13. Was that the extent of your training, doctor?
14. Where did you train for your specialty?
15. How long did such training take?
16. What was the nature of the training?
17. After that, what did you do?

18. What type of practice have you engaged in since that time?

19. What is neurology?

20. Doctor, would you please tell us the names of the medical societies of which you are a member?

21. Are you, or have you been, on the staff of any medical school?

22. Doctor, tell us please, the names of the hospitals with which you are associated in a staff capacity.

23. Are you board certified in your specialty of neurology?

24. What does that board certification mean?

25. Is this a National Board that's given by your colleagues?

26. Do you have to practice for a certain number of years before you take a written exam?

27. What societies do you belong to, doctor, in connection with your profession?

28. Thank you, doctor. Now, have you had a patient by the name of *Henrietta Hurt?*

29. Do you have Mrs. Hurt's office records, regarding her treatment and care in front of you at this time?

30. Please feel free to refer to those notes and records to refresh your memory if necessary.

31. Will you please tell us the date of your first examination of Mrs. Hurt?

32. Since the date of your initial examination of Mrs. Hurt, has she continued to be your patient?

33. When did you last see Mrs. Hurt as a patient?

34. How frequently have you seen her?

35. On how many separate occasions have you examined or treated Mrs. Hurt?

36. Was Mrs. Hurt referred to you as a patient?

37. By whom was she referred?

38. Have you discharged Mrs. Hurt as a patient?

39. Did you refer Mrs. Hurt to Doctor Blessum?

40. At the time of your first examination of Mrs. Hurt, did you give her a neurological examination?

41. What did that consist of?

42. Did you obtain a history from the patient at that time?

43. Doctor, is a history important to you as a neurologist?

44. What is the reason for that?

45. Will you relate to us the history that Mrs. Hurt gave you at the time of your initial examination of her?

46. At the time of your initial examination, did the patient complain of pain?

47. Will you describe her complaints?

48. Did she have any other complaints?

49. What did you do after hearing the patient's history and complaints?

50. Doctor, did you discern any abnormality in her neck other than what she told you? In other words, were there any objective signs to support the subjective complaints (i.e., examination)?

51. Doctor, please explain the difference between objective and subjective complaints.

52. You will be asked to explain any medical terms regarding certain muscles, etc., that may be confusing to the jury (e.g., *trapezius, nucleus pulposus*).

53. After hearing the patient's history and complaints, did you examine her?

54. Will you tell us what portions of the Plaintiff's body you examined and the various tests you gave her, keeping in mind that the jury and I are laypeople, and using language we can understand?

55. Please explain what tests you recommended that she have performed.

56. After your examining Mrs. Hurt, did you suggest that she have X rays taken of the neck, etc.? (The same questions may be asked relative to MRIs, CAT scans, or other applicable tests.)

57. Were those X rays taken here in your office?

58. Did you review those X rays, doctor?

59. What is your opinion concerning the results of those X rays regarding fractures or dislocations?

60. If the X rays are normal, does that mean that there are no fractures and dislocations?

61. Does that necessarily rule out any muscle involvement?

62. Does it mean that there is no soft tissue injury?

63. Does it negate any nerve impingement?

64. Does it mean that there are no vascular injuries?

65. In other words, if the X rays were normal as to fracture and dislocations, it does not necessarily mean that there is no involvement in the other components of the neck such as soft tissue, muscles, and ligaments, does it?

66. Doctor, after taking a history of the patient, examining her, and obtaining X rays, did you make a diagnosis? What diagnosis?

67. Doctor, do you have an opinion, based on a reasonable degree of medical probability, as to whether or not the injuries that you diagnosed as to Mrs. Hurt were caused by the automobile accident of January 7, 1992?

68. And what is that opinion?

69. After making the diagnosis, doctor, what did you do to treat her for her injuries?

70. Did she, in fact, go through a regimen of physical therapy at your suggestion?

71. Could you describe for us the treatment that she undertook, and where she was treated?

72. Discuss each of the subsequent visits and whether she was examined on such occasions. Discuss the results of each examination.

73. Pursuant to such examinations, what did you feel her clinical course held for her?

74. Doctor, what treatment did you prescribe for her in the hospital?

75. Did she improve as a result of this treatment?

76. What did you do then, if anything?

77. Doctor, please tell us the results of Mrs. Hurt's treatment in the hospital.

78. When, if ever, will Mrs. Hurt be in the same condition of health she was in prior to her injury with respect to her cervical spine?

79. Based on a reasonable medical certainty, can you fix an approximate range within which Mrs. Hurt's disability will extend as a result of this injury to her cervical spine?

80. To what extent, if any, will Mrs. Hurt be able to resume heavy housework?

81. Discuss whether she will be restricted in any of her other activities.

82. Doctor, do you feel that the injuries that you described have been a source of pain for Mrs. Hurt in the past?

83. Is that opinion based on reasonable medical probability?

84. Do you have an opinion, doctor, based on reasonable degree of medical probability as to whether or not she can expect some pain in the future from these injuries that you described?

85. Doctor, do you have an opinion based on reasonable medical probability whether Mrs. Hurt's injuries sustained in this accident physically disabled her to the point that she was unable to work?

86. What is the extent of her disability rating?

87. Doctor, do you have an opinion based on reasonable medical probability whether Mrs. Hurt's injuries sustained in this accident impaired her ability to work and do the usual tasks of a working person?

88. What is that opinion?

89. Did Mrs. Hurt appear to be depressed or despondent as a result of her injuries?

90. Doctor, during the course of your treatment to date, was Mrs. Hurt restricted from engaging in any of her normal activities outside her work, such as hobbies, social activities, etc.?

91. Doctor, do you have an opinion within reasonable medical probability as to whether this impairment that you have just described will continue into the future?

92. Doctor, do you have a bill for the services that you provided for Mrs. Hurt?

93. What is the total bill?

94. Do you have a copy of this bill?

95. Doctor, are you familiar with the fair and reasonable charges for medical services of the nature that you have described here in Bexar County, Texas?

96. Do you have an opinion as to whether (state amount) is the fair and reasonable charge for the services that your offices provided to Mrs. Hurt and as to whether or not the current treatment afforded her by your office was necessary for the treatment of the injuries that she sustained in the automobile collision described? What is that opinion?

97. Did you prescribe any prescription drugs for Mrs. Hurt? What did you prescribe and what is its purpose?

98. Are you familiar with hospital charges in this area? Do you consider the charges to Mrs. Hurt in the amount of $______ to be reasonable and necessary charges for Bexar County, Texas.

99. Doctor, do you anticipate that Mrs. Hurt will need any medical treatment in the future, whether from a neurosurgeon, physical therapist, or other doctor, as well as any pharmaceuticals, physical therapy, or other treatment, based on reasonable medical probability?

100. Doctor, please estimate approximately how much the future medical care and treatment will cost.

Note: additional questions may be required to obtain the admissibility of documents and records. See the questioning in Chapter 6 relative to Laying Foundations for a partial example.

Cross-Examination. The conduct of cross-examination has the same purposes as it has with any other witness, that is to discredit the witness or minimize the impact of the testimony. Frequently a major focus in cross-examination pertains to the patient's medical records. For example, negative findings such as no broken bones, normal X rays, and full range of motion will be pointed out by the cross-examiner.

EXAMPLE

Q: Dr. isn't it true that your records do not show any complaints of restriction of motion in the shoulder area?

It is also probable that any inconsistencies in the applicable medical records will be discovered by the cross-examiner and will form the basis of additional questions.

Another major area of concentration on cross-examination is further exploration of points raised on direct examination. The effort here is to ask penetrating questions discrediting or confining the impact of statements previously made.

EXAMPLE

Q: Isn't it entirely possible that this injury could have been caused by something other than this accident?

Q: Doctor you didn't witness this accident on February 24, 1992, did you?

Q: And, your knowledge of what happened there is confined solely to what Mrs. Hurt told you, isn't it?

Q: So, in fact, you're relying on what she has told you as to how she was really hurt?

If your client's attorney used a hypothetical question on direct examination it is likely that the cross-examiner will ask you questions calculated to attack the assumptions given in the hypothetical question. Even if hypothetical questions were not used on direct examination do not be surprised if your cross-examiner resorts to this method. The cross-examiners objective will be to obtain your concession that your opinion would be modified if their hypothesis is correct and thereby create doubt in the minds of the jurors.

EXAMPLE

Q: Doctor, you were asked during direct examination, to assume as true a number of premises and based on those premises you rendered an opinion that the cause of plaintiff's illness was her exposure to the pesticide Ridarat, did you not?

A: Yes, I did.

Q: Now, Doctor, would it change your opinion if in addition to the premises stated during the posing of that question, you added the fact that . . .

Q: Doctor, if you were aware of this additional information isn't it true that your opinion as to the cause of plaintiffs present illness, in all reasonable medical probability, arises not from her exposure to the pesticide Ridarat but due to these additional circumstances.

Handwriting Experts and Questioned Document Analysis

Handwriting experts, like people, come in all sizes and shapes. More to the point, since handwriting analysis is not a well-established profession, it is more difficult to separate the qualified from the unqualified expert. For this reason, the qualification questions are a crucial part of the direct examination of handwriting experts. In addition to the usual background questions, handwriting experts should be prepared to advise (1) how long they have been engaged in such work, (2) how many documents they have rendered opinions on, and (3) how many times they have testified in court.

After the witness has been qualified, the direct examination will proceed along the following lines:

Q: I hand you what has been marked as Exhibit B and ask whether you have had occasion to study and examine this exhibit prior to coming to court today.
Q: At whose request did you perform this examination?
Q: When and where did your examination take place?
Q: Who else was present during the examination?
Q: What was the purpose of your examination?
Q: How did you go about conducting your examination?
Q: As a result of your examination, were you able to arrive at a conclusion as to the authenticity of the signature of Sam Scribble?
Q: What is that conclusion?
Q: Please tell the jury in detail how you arrived at that conclusion.

> ***Practice Tip:*** **Because of this field's graphic nature, handwriting experts should prepare enlarged photographic reproductions of the exhibits to illustrate their findings to the jury. These exhibits will also provide convincing evidence for jurors in conducting their deliberations.**

Engineers

In addition to the usual rules and questions applying to all expert witnesses, engineers are subject to a variety of questions relating to the technical nature of the case and their precise area of expertise. The expansion of product liability litigation in the past 25 years has significantly increased the involvement of engineers, of all types, as expert witnesses in the civil courts.

The following list reflects the general areas of interrogation of an engineer:

1. *Materials Provided for Review*

EXAMPLES

Q: Please tell us each and every item of information you have reviewed in this case.

Q: Are you expecting to obtain additional records?

2. *Verbal Information*

EXAMPLES

Q: What information has been related to you by other persons and by whom?

Q: Have you made any written notations of this information?

Q: Have you relied on this information in formulating your opinion? To what extent?

3. *Official Standards and Tables*

EXAMPLES

Q: What are the sources?

Q: What was the information used for?

Q: Who obtained the information?

Q: Is the information commonly relied on by others in the industry?

4. *The Specific Product Involved*

EXAMPLES

Q: Have you examined the product?
Q: When and where?
Q: What tests were performed?
Q: How was the product obtained?
Q: What is the chain of custody of the product from the time of the accident to the present?

5. *Industry Standards*

EXAMPLES

Q: What industry standards were applied in performing your work?
Q: Are these standards generally relied on in the industry?
Q: Do other experts in the field accept this theory?

6. *The Purpose of the Expert's Work*

EXAMPLES

Q: What were you asked to do?
Q: What did you do?
Q: Have you done it before?
Q: How did you set about doing it?

7. *Results*

EXAMPLES

Q: What findings were made?
Q: How were they arrived at?
Q: What is the significance of your findings?
Q: How reliable are they?
Q: What equipment was used in your work?

8. *Conclusion*

EXAMPLES

Q: What are your opinions based on your findings?

Q: What facts were relied on in arriving at your conclusions?

Q: Does anything else need to be done to finalize your work?

Q: Could your opinion change?

9. *Terms and Jargon.* Explain all technical terms to the jury. Make it simple and understandable.

10. *Reasoning.* Your findings, factual bases and opinions must all tie together. A causal relationship must be established.

While the preceding queries illustrate the type of inquiries that will be made, the precise wording of the question will vary depending on whether direct examination or cross-examination is being pursued.

The following is a brief list of typical inqurries of an engineering expert on direct examination in a products liability case.

Q: Were you able to form any opinions as whether this product had any design, manufacturing, or marketing defects?

Q: Did you form any opinions as to whether there was a causal relationship between any defects you found and the plaintiff's injuries?

Q: Do you have an opinion as to whether the defects you found, if any, were the producing cause of plaintiff's injury?

Q: What materials did you review and what tests did you perform to arrive at your opinions?

Q: Are you aware of any other claims against this manufacturer where the same product has resulted in similar accidents?

Q: Do you know of any changes made in the design of this product after this accident occurred?

Q: Do you have an opinion in reasonable scientific probability as to whether the defendant had preexisting knowledge of the unreasonably dangerous design of this product?

Fire Loss Experts

In fire loss litigation or fire insurance claims, the expertise of arson investigators, fire marshals, contractors, and other such experts becomes essential. In such instances, the degree of experience in investigation of the cause and origin of fires is a critical factor for qualification. The key to qualification as an expert witness is a special knowledge and experience in fire loss investigation beyond the common knowledge of jurors. The facts of the case will have a bearing on the precise degree and type of training and experience that will be necessary for qualification.

Fire cases provide an excellent opportunity for the use of diagrams, photographs, and other such visual aids. Expert witnesses should be prepared with such exhibits and should use them liberally in their presentation to the jury. In making a presentation, fire loss experts should be thoroughly familiar with the fire scene and the applicable investigation file. It is important to explain to the jury in chronological order all the steps involved in the fire loss investigation. In some instances, it may be helpful to prepare an outline organizing all the names, dates and other pertinent facts so that the presentation will flow well.

Establishing Fire Damages Through Contractors. The following list exemplifies the basic questions used to establish fire repair costs through the testimony of a building contractor.

Q: State your name, address, etc.
Q: What is your occupation?
Q: How long have you been so engaged?
Q: What type of building have you done?
Q: Describe your professional activities and experiences for the court and jury.
Q: Where has your business been located?
A: Mostly Bexar County, Texas.
Q: Are you familiar with the cost of building materials in the vicinity of Bexar County, Texas?
Q: Are you familiar with the fair market value of labor of the type employed in the building trades in the vicinity of Bexar County, Texas?
Q: Are you familiar with the property involved in this action, the Los Arboles Apartments?
Q: Have you examined this property?
Q: When did you do so?
Q: What was the purpose of the examination?
A: I was requested to prepare an estimate of the cost of repairs to restore the property to the condition it was in prior to the fire.
Q: In making your examination of the property what items of damage did you find?
Q: What in your opinion would be the reasonable cost of materials and fair market value of labor necessary in making the repairs to this property?
Q: Do you consider these figures to be reasonable and necessary cost of repairs in Bexar County, Texas?
Q: If these repairs were made what would be the value of the property as compared with its value before the fire?
A: It will be basically the same.

Typical Deposition Questions of Fire Department Officials in Fire Cases. The following is an example of the questioning scenario at the deposition of a fire department official:

1. Please state your full name for the record.
2. Where do you reside?
3. How long have you been a resident of San Antonio?
4. What is your age?
5. What is your occupation or profession?
6. How long have you been employed by the Fire Department?
7. As a District Chief, what are your responsibilities and duties?
8. Would you please give us a little summary of what your training and experience has been? [Proper follow up questions will be asked to enable you to qualify as an expert witness on fire causation.]
9. Tell us during this period of time when you first started and as you progressed up through the ranks, what kind of duties were required of you and what duties did you perform?
10. What does a fireman do when not fighting fires?
11. What training have you received in fire origin investigation, fire fighting, and fire safety from the time you started until now?
12. How many individuals are under your supervision?
13. You are what is called a District Chief?
14. How many District Chiefs are in the City?
15. Whom do you report to?
16. During this period of time when you have been coming up through the ranks, has it been necessary for you to take and pass certain tests to go to the next level?
17. About how many times have you been promoted?
18. Now, let me direct your attention and see if you had occasion to supervise the control of a fire that occurred on ____________ at ____________?
19. Will you tell us what was the occasion for your going there and how you were notified and so forth?

20. At about what time of day or night was this?

21. Was the fire already in progress at the time you got there?

22. Tell us what you found or the condition that you found the premises in then and what happened there later on until the fire was put out. (Appropriate follow up questions will be asked to get details.)

23. Did you go in and inspect the premises on the inside or look at it before you left?

24. Was that part of your duties?

25. Tell us what you found on the inside of the house when you viewed the premises there. (Additional questions will be asked to develop details.)

26. What type of structure was this? (Size, number of floors, type of construction, etc.)

27. Generally an attempt will be made to introduce the fire report into evidence by asking the appropriate questions to qualify it as either a business record exception to the Hearsay Rule or as a public record.

Cross-Examination. The following list shows the areas of inquiry that a cross-examiner might probe in a fire loss caused by a defective furnace or improper installation depending on the extent to which they were discussed in direct examination:

1. Who the expert was hired by. (To show bias, if any.)
2. Number of trips made to investigate the product or scene of the fire and dates thereof.
3. Introduction of the expert's report as an exhibit.
4. Inquiries as to other documents or memoranda the expert had prepared or possesses, (e.g., notes, color slides, laboratory tests), using them as a basis for more detailed questioning.
5. Information relative to the age of the product and how long it had been in use.

6. The date of loss in relation to the date of expert's first inspection.
7. A determination of where the loss actually occurred and what additional damage was viewed by the expert in the general area where the loss occurred.
8. Inquiries as to what the expert was told about the fire or loss before making the inspection.
9. Length of time spent on inspection, and identification of anybody else who was present.
10. Questions relative to where the fire originated (in specific detail).
11. Facts relied on by the expert in determining fire origin.
12. Evidence of anything else in the area of the product where the fire started that could have caused the loss.
13. Proximity of the product to the closest combustible material and naming of the closest combustible material.
14. Determination of whether the wiring in the area where the fire occurred was inspected.
15. Effect of fire on any wiring.
16. Detailed description of what wiring existed there.
17. Explanation of any history or background on the use of the product given to the expert prior to inspection and/or report.
18. Determination of whether the product controls were damaged or destroyed by the fire. Usually if the product is available, extensive questioning will take place while it is being viewed.
19. Whether at the time of the inspection, the expert noticed anything unusual about the product assembly. (If photos were taken, were they taken before the product was moved for further inspection?)
20. Specific details relative to burn patterns, charring, and other details used in determining origin of fire and whether certain factors existed prior to or subsequent to the loss.

21. A determination of whether the evidence reflects fire damage, etc., from within the product or whether it appeared to be from an exterior source of fire.

22. A determination of whether the expert has given all the physical evidence and observations gathered at the time of the first inspection.

23. Information regarding each subsequent inspection in terms of date and results.

24. Who was present at each of the inspections by the expert.

25. A determination as to the expert's knowledge of anyone else who viewed the product either in the expert's presence or otherwise.

26. Who removed the product from the premises or area of the loss.

27. Inquiries whether any alleged designed effects, etc., that were observed by the expert were, in his/her opinion, peculiar to that particular product or in the alternative, that type of product.

28. Determination of whether the defect or problem would have been visible to an alert observer.

29. If so, determination of whether the dangers of the condition would be obvious to such observer.

30. Details regarding the expert's inspection of the product, including the nature of the inspection, how it was done, and how long it took.

The foregoing subjects are representative only. The precise subject areas and nature of questions will vary depending on whether the questioning is on deposition discovery or at trial. Obviously if the inquiries are detailed at deposition, the trial questioning is likely to be less extensive and more focused on the key areas.

Accountants and Other Economists

The use of economists as expert witnesses to provide damage testimony in serious personal injury cases has had a remarkable impact. Such testimony frequently enables a jury to envision much greater damages than may otherwise be the case.

Direct Examination. The following list summarizes the substance of direct examination of the accountant or economist as an expert witness for the plaintiff in a personal injury case.

1. *Functions of Economists.* Kinds of services provided (i.e.: evaluate economic loss resulting from injury or death, prepare statistics, calculate present values); users of these services (i.e.: banks, accountants, attorneys, government, real estate industry).
2. *Education and Training of Economists.* May include description of college education, advanced degrees, training in mathematics, statistics, research, and related areas.
3. *Economic Terms and Concepts.* Expert's discussion and explanation in lay language of applicable economic terms and concepts (e.g., economic forecasting, present value discount, inflation rates, wage scales); explanation of all charts, graphs, and other visual aids.
4. *Expert's Involvement in the Case.* Calculation of present value discounts, determination of loss of wage earnings, wage-earning capacity, value of fringe benefits, etc.
5. *Information Provided to Expert in This Case.* Facts about the case, details on plaintiff's background, documents, pleadings, work records, insurance policies, personnel files, etc.
6. *Other Sources of Information.* Government bulletins, mortality tables, statistical publications, etc.
7. *Determinations Made by Expert.* Results and opinions. Damage determinations.

8. *Methods of Arriving at Those Determinations.* Use of inflation factors, interest rate tables, discount factors, and other calculations and computations.
9. *Facts, Assumptions, and Projections Relied on to Reach the Determinations.* Facts of case, assumptions as to life style, interest rates, life expectancy, tax rates, etc.
10. *Hypothetical Questions.* In some cases, much of the foregoing can be arranged in a hypothetical question as to expert's opinion based on reasonable economic probability.

Cross-Examination. The precise thrust of cross-examination will depend on what is covered on direct examination and what are perceived to be the weak spots or questionable areas. As pointed out in Chapter 7, all experts are subject to attack relative to their experience, track record, or other qualifications.

However, in addition to those general areas of questioning, economists can expect to be interrogated in great detail on the following subject areas:

1. *Uncertainty of Predicting the Future.* The objective here is to point out the foibles of forecasting or predicting the future in an effort to cause the jury to question the reliability of your determinations. This is accomplished by illustrating the reliance on assumptions, and projections both as to the past and the future. For example, do your determinations assume that technology, employment standards, and other such factors will remain the same? Do your determinations take into account the effects of possible future events such as wars, depressions, etc.? Can you guarantee the future? To what extent have you utilized averages in making your determinations? All these areas demonstrate the possible uncertainty involved and how it can bring the reliability of your determinations into question.
2. *Dependability of Sources of Information Used.* The cross-examiner will be looking at information you relied on in

your work. If there are exaggerations in the basic data, it undermines the entire project. (For example, if you are testifying as to the monetary value of the household services of a spouse, did the family exaggerate the amount of hours the spouse had expended each week providing such services? If so, doesn't that jeopardize the accuracy of all your results?)

The following are some questions that might be asked to attack your sources of information.

EXAMPLES

Q: Have you ever talked with the plaintiffs personally in preparing your work?

Q: How many hours did you spend just with their attorneys in preparing your testimony?

Q: Doesn't the life expectancy table just deal with averages?

Q: Did you ever see the decedent's tax returns and financial information or did you just rely on what the client's lawyer told you?

Q: Have you ever reviewed medical reports to document your assumptions as to the plaintiff's disability or are you just accepting that as fact?

3. *Accuracy of Projections and Assumptions.* You can expect extensive examination in these areas. The following are typical problem areas.

EXAMPLES

Q: In projecting the plaintiff's future income potential, did you consider the possibility of:

a. Premature death

b. Changes in working conditions such as layoffs, strikes, etc.

c. Illnesses or other potential disabilities

d. Macroeconomic conditions in general?

Q: In preparing your projections, did you make all your assumptions in favor of plaintiff?

Q: Didn't you assume that the plaintiff would remain in good health, steadily at work until retirement and with a continuing increase of salary and fringe benefits?

Q: Don't these assumptions disregard the effects of strikes, recessions, temporary illness, etc.?

Q: Did you take into account the effect of income and FICA taxes as to actual take-home pay?

Q: In making your determinations as to the value of Mrs. Doe's household services, have you taken into consideration the changing family requirements after the children are grown and gone?

In addition to the foregoing, the following areas represent additional opportunities for the accounting expert:

- *Probate Courts.* To value business interests or trace assets
- *Real Estate Matters.* To value property for condemnation cases or determination of damages in contract cases
- *Divorce Cases.* Tracing of assets, determination of business interests, calculation of support arrangements
- *Bankruptcy.* Tracing, valuations, cash flow computations and related matters

Obviously the opportunities are not limited to the above examples. The point is that there are abundant litigation opportunities for the experienced and court wise accountant.

WITNESS CHARACTERISTICS

In Chapter 7, we discussed common characteristics and techniques of trial lawyers, particularly with reference to cross-examination. The personalities and characteristics of expert witnesses also need study because they affect the interchange with trial lawyers on cross-examination. More importantly, some insight into the problems or results of certain witness characteristics can be a catalyst for future development and improvement. It is certainly worth your time to peruse the following characteristics and determine what application they may have for your performance and success.

- *The Windbag.* This person won't stop talking. This is often a basic personality trait and difficult to change. However, this trait is not compatible with expert witness work and can get you into trouble. Most cross-examiners will hold you in tight rein and limit your responses, but they can get lots of mileage out of what you said at deposition or on direct examination. Long-winded responses waste time, create unnecessary problems on cross-examination, and frequently alienate you from the jury. If you have a tendency in this direction work on it by trying to be thorough but concise. Be responsive but don't provide unrequested information.
- *The Clam.* This witness is basically the opposite of the windbag. This trait causes more problems for your own lawyer than it does the cross-examiner. Dragging information out of you can be difficult for the attorney. It makes the direct examination exceedingly tedious and generally impairs its effectiveness with the jury.

  Remember your job is to provide the jury with important convincing information that supports your client's position. To accomplish this effectively, you must provide sufficiently detailed responses to support your position.
- *The Nerd.* The nerd is dull, dull, dull. If this is you, learn how to pizazz it up. You cannot possibly impress the jury with your findings if they aren't listening to you. The ability to make your testimony somewhat interesting to the jury is a key goal for testifying expert witnesses.
- *The Contemplator.* This witness is not necessarily dull, but you can fall asleep waiting to hear what the individual is

going to say. In trial work, you don't have that luxury. Although it is often fine to take your time and think before you respond, you don't want to go over the edge. If you take too long, your testimony will lose its spontaneity and will be unconvincing. Extreme time lapses between questions and answers lend an impression of uncertainty or lack of knowledge.

- *The Show-Off.* This witness purveys a know-it-all attitude that can be immediately offensive to the jurors. Additionally, the courtroom is no place for exaggerated gestures, or body language. Likewise, your speech should be natural and responsive. The show-off attempts to make the courtroom a stage. Unfortunately, this not only appears ridiculous but hurts the client's case.
- *The Affable Agreer.* The affable agreer tends to be everyone's friend. This may make you a likable person, but it can get you into lots of trouble in the courtroom. Successful expert witnesses have to be able to stand their ground and disagree where appropriate. Witnesses who agree with every statement made by the cross-examiner will find themselves in "deep yogurt," very quickly. You must have the courage of your convictions.
- *The Analyst.* This witness gets too bogged down in the details. The key to success in jury trials is to keep it as simple as possible. Jurors do not want to be overeducated. This witness also tends to overanalyze everything. This frequently results in noncommittal or qualified responses such as "to the best of my recollection," which deaden the impact of the testimony with the jury. This type of witness should work on simply responding straightforwardly to the questions instead of analyzing them into the ground.
- *The Deep Freezer.* These individuals become as solidly frozen as an ice cube when required to take center stage. In the witness box, they are the focus of everyone's attention and are under the additional stress of the courtroom controversy. Witnesses who suffer from stage fright become like the clam with

similar results. The bright side is that stage fright may be only a temporary condition and can be worked through. More importantly, it can be worked on in advance by familiarizing yourself with the courtroom scenario. A trial run of your testimony with your client's lawyers can also add to your comfort and confidence.

HEARSAY

As you may have noted, hearsay has been discussed several times earlier in this book. The hearsay rules are quite comprehensive and can be complex in application. Accordingly, a general knowledge of the formal Rules of Evidence governing the use and application of hearsay is important to attorneys and expert witnesses alike. Article VIII of the Federal Rules of Evidence sets forth six pertinent rules (Rules 801–806). Knowing these rules will help you understand what is or is not admissible evidence and why.

Rule 801—Definitions

1. *Statement.* An oral or written assertion or any other nonverbal conduct that is intended as an assertion.
2. *Declarant.* A person who makes a statement (as previously defined).
3. *Hearsay.* A *statement* being offered in evidence as proof; does not apply to statements made in the courtroom while testifying. "The doctor told me" is hearsay; however, for the doctor to come into the courtroom and tell what he said to the patient is not hearsay.)
4. *Statements That Are Not Hearsay.*
   a. Prior statement by witness—prior statements made in the case under oath may be admitted to impeach or support the present testimony of the witness.

b. Admission by party opponent—statements made by or attributable to a party in a lawsuit are admissible against them as an exception to the hearsay rule.

Both of these types of statement are likely to be offered on cross-examination, not direct examination.

Rule 802—Hearsay Rule

This states the general rule that hearsay (as defined in the previous rule) is not admissible.

Rule 803—Hearsay Exceptions: Availability of Declarant Immaterial

This rule provides 24 exceptions to the hearsay rule. All these exceptions are in fact hearsay but are still admissible as evidence. Attorneys rely on knowledge of these exceptions to determine what will or will not be admissible. For this reason, a general knowledge of the 24 hearsay exceptions will be useful to the expert witness. Appendix I presents Rule 803 in its entirety.

Rule 804—Hearsay Exceptions; Declarant Unavailable

This rule lists five (5) additional exceptions to the hearsay rule, applicable when the declarant making the statement is unavailable to testify in open court because of:

1. A court ruling that has exempted the witness from testifying on the basis of privilege.
2. A refusal to testify.
3. A lack of memory.
4. Inability to testify because of death, mental illness, or infirmity.

5. Absence of witness combined with an unsuccessful effort to compel attendance through service of process or other reasonable means.

> ***Practice Tip:*** **To utilize the Rule 804 exceptions to get evidence admitted, the proponent must satisfy the court that the admission of such statements is in the best interest of seeing justice served. The proponent must also show that the opposition was notified in advance of trial, of the intent to rely on such evidence so the opposition will have a fair opportunity to react and respond. See Appendix I for the full text of Rule 804.**

Rule 805—Hearsay Within Hearsay

Hearsay included within hearsay is not excluded under the hearsay rule if each part of the combined statements conforms with an exception to the hearsay rule, otherwise provided for in the rules.

Rule 806—Attacking and Supporting Credibility of Declarant

Since Rule 801 specifies that certain statements are not considered hearsay and may therefore be allowed, this rule provides the opposing party an opportunity to attack the declarant's credibility in the same manner as if the individual had appeared in court to make the statements.

USEFUL QUESTIONS AND ANSWERS

How soon can I destroy file materials after the conclusion of a case?

You should never destroy file material as long as the case is still subject to appeal or reopening. In addition, you should find out from your client's attorney whether there are any laws in the applicable jurisdiction relative to file retention.

You should maintain any accounting, expense, or timekeeping records for at least three (3) years in the event of any IRS audits. Personally, I prefer to keep all file materials for at least 3 to 5 years just in case of any unforeseen need. I also find that I am constantly referring back to closed files for useful information.

Is it proper to purge your file of notes or harmful information prior to discovery?

Once you are designated as a testifying expert, your file materials are subject to discovery. You should therefore, consolidate your material down to only the organized, favorable, and useful information. Although you are obligated to tell the truth on all matters, you are not obligated to hang on to negative notes or observations you may have made in the process of preparing your case. As a general rule, the less paper you have in your file the better.

What is a reasonable fee?

As discussed in Chapter 3, the hourly fee is the prevalent measure of compensation for an expert witness. Although you are certainly entitled to be well compensated, too many testifying experts attempt to take advantage of the system. A person with a standard education who happens to have significant experience in a subject area at issue should not be paid the same hourly rate as the highly educated professional or attorney just because that is what the traffic will bear. If you are customarily compensated at the rate of $20 per hour being paid $100 per hour to testify in court may be unfair. You may be entitled to a premium, but be wary of overreaching.

If you are already on a salary or working out of your home with virtually no overhead, I personally would find it hard to justify paying you an hourly rate in excess of $100 per hour. On the other hand, if you are a highly compensated professional or have substantial overhead, then a higher rate may be acceptable. The bottom line is to strive to be fair and reasonable and avoid the temptation to "gouge out" what the traffic will bear.

What do I do if I am contacted by both sides of the litigation?

When you are first contacted, you will need to determine promptly whether you are going to work for that party in the case. Once you have agreed to represent one party, it would be improper to later represent the other party even if you later drop or are dropped from representation of the first party. Until you are actually engaged by one party or the other, however, you do have some latitude as to which side you represent in the case. Unless the first party to contact you conveys privileged or confidential information, it would be possible to decline representation and later accept representation by the other party if they were to contact you. You should be extremely careful about this, however, since you do not want to make any decisions that give the slightest indication of being unfair or unethical. If there is any doubt, the best step is simply to stay out of it altogether.

What do I do if I get into a case and disagree with my client's position?

You have an obligation to express your opinions fairly and impartially to your client. If you fudge on your determinations you are headed for trouble. Once you have informed your client, let the attorneys decide whether they want to continue your services as a consulting expert (rather than testifying expert) or terminate the services. Do not commit anything to writing unless you are asked to do so by the client.

What do I do if my client's attorney fails to do an effective job of preparing, assisting, or informing me?

If you are able to determine this fairly early on, you may want to get out of the case. If it is too late to fairly consider that, the only remaining alternative is to work extra hard to prepare yourself as thoroughly as possible. Document your requests of the attorney in writing, then do as much as you possibly can to be prepared on the law and legal issues, as well as the facts of the case.

What if the client fails to pay my monthly bill?

If you are not paid, you should immediately demand a payment deadline, if you are not paid by that date, reject any further work in the matter. To avoid serious problems in this regard, you should obtain appropriate advance retainers and stay current on payment for your services as rendered.

Will it limit my effectiveness if I am a full-time testifying witness?

Not necessarily. While it may enhance your credibility with the jury if you are a working professional in your field of expertise, you still have plenty to offer when you devote yourself fully to consulting and testifying on a given subject. You should, however, make a concerted effort to avoid any appearance of being a hired gun. Be prepared to show the time you spend on writing, teaching, lecturing, studying, or other such activities besides testifying in court.

What should I do if an emergency arises when I am scheduled for deposition or a court appearance?

Obviously, your duty is to keep your commitments whenever possible even if it is inconvenient. However, in the event of a true emergency, you should immediately contact your (client's) lawyer and explain the situation. The burden will really fall on the lawyer to make the necessary rearrangements or improvisation.

APPENDIX I

Excerpts from the Rules of Evidence Concerning Hearsay (Article VIII)

RULE 803. HEARSAY EXCEPTIONS; AVAILABILITY OF DECLARANT IMMATERIAL

The following are not excluded by the hearsay rule, even though the declarant is available as a witness:

(1) Present Sense Impression. A statement describing or explaining an event or condition made while the declarant was perceiving the event or condition, or immediately thereafter.

(2) Excited Utterance. A statement relating to a startling event or condition made while the declarant was under the stress of excitement caused by the event or condition.

(3) Then Existing Mental, Emotional, or Physical Condition. A statement of the declarant's then existing state of mind, emotion, sensation, or physical condition (such as intent, plan, motive, design, mental feeling, pain, and bodily health), but not including a statement of memory or belief to prove the fact remembered or believed unless it relates to the execution, revocation, identification, or terms of declarant's will.

(4) Statements for Purposes of Medical Diagnosis or Treatment. Statements made for purposes of medical diagnosis or treatment and describing medical history, or past or present symptoms, pain, or sensations, or the inception or general character of the cause or external source thereof insofar as reasonably pertinent to diagnosis or treatment.

(5) Recorded Recollection. A memorandum or record concerning a matter about which a witness once had knowledge but now has insufficient recollection to enable the witness to testify fully and accurately, shown to have been made or adopted by the witness when the matter was fresh in the witness' memory and to reflect that knowledge correctly. If admitted, the memorandum or record may be read into evidence but may not itself be received as an exhibit unless offered by an adverse party.

(6) Records of Regularly Conducted Activity. A memorandum, report, record, or data compilation, in any form, of acts, events, conditions, opinions, or diagnoses, made at or near the time by, or from information transmitted by, a person with knowledge, if kept in the course of a regularly conducted business activity, and if it was the regular practice of that business activity to make the memorandum, report, record, or data compilation, all as shown by the testimony of the custodian or other qualified witness, unless the source of information or the method or circumstances of preparation indicate lack of trustworthiness. The term "business" as used in this paragraph includes business, institution, association, profession, occupation, and calling of every kind, whether or not conducted for profit.

(7) Absence of Entry in Records Kept in Accordance with the Provisions of Paragraph (6). Evidence that a matter is not included in the memoranda reports, records, or data compilations, in any form, kept in accordance with the provisions of paragraph (6), to prove the nonoccurrence or nonexistence of the matter, if the matter was of a kind of which a memorandum, report, record, or data compilation was regularly made and preserved, unless the sources of information or other circumstances indicate lack of trustworthiness.

(8) Public Records and Reports. Records, reports, statements, or data compilations, in any form, of public offices or agencies, setting forth (A) the activities of the office or agency, or (B) matters observed pursuant to duty imposed by law as to which matters there was a duty to report, excluding, however, in criminal cases matters observed by police officers and other law enforcement personnel, or (C) in civil actions and proceedings and against the Government in criminal cases, factual findings resulting from an investigation made pursuant to authority granted by law, unless the sources of information or other circumstances indicate lack of trustworthiness.

(9) Records of Vital Statistics. Records or data compilations, in any form, of births, fetal deaths, deaths, or marriages, if the report thereof was made to a public office pursuant to requirements of law.

(10) Absence of Public Record or Entry. To prove the absence of a record, report, statement, or data compilation, in any form, or the nonoccurrence or nonexistence of a matter of which a record, report, statement, or data compilation, in any form, was regularly made and preserved by a public office or agency, evidence in the form of a certification in accordance with rule 902, or testimony, that diligent search failed to disclose the record, report, statement, or data compilation, or entry.

(11) Records of Religious Organizations. Statements of births, marriages, divorces, deaths, legitimacy, ancestry, relationship by blood or marriage, or other similar facts of personal or family history, contained in a regularly kept record of a religious organization.

(12) Marriage, Baptismal, and Similar Certificates. Statements of fact contained in a certificate that the maker performed a marriage or other ceremony or administered a sacrament, made by a clergyman, public official, or other person authorized by the rules or practices of a religious organization or by law to perform the act certified, and purporting to have been issued at the time of the act or within a reasonable time thereafter.

(13) Family Records. Statements of fact concerning personal or family history contained in family Bibles, genealogies, charts, engravings on rings, inscriptions on family portraits, engravings on urns, crypts, or tombstones, or the like.

(14) Records of Documents Affecting an Interest in Property. The record of a document purporting to establish or affect an interest in property, as proof of the content of the original recorded document and its execution and delivery by each person by whom it purports to have been executed, if the record is a record of a public office and an applicable statute authorizes the recording of documents of that kind in that office.

(15) Statements in Documents Affecting an Interest in Property. A statement contained in a document purporting to establish or affect an interest in property if the matter stated was relevant to the purpose of the document, unless dealings with the property since the document was made have been inconsistent with the truth of the statement or the purport of the document.

(16) Statements in Ancient Documents. Statements in a document in existence twenty years or more the authenticity of which is established.

(17) Market Reports, Commercial Publications. Market quotations, tabulations, lists, directories, or other published compilations, generally used and relied upon by the public or by persons in particular occupations.

(18) Learned Treatises. To the extent called to the attention of an expert witness upon cross-examination or relied upon by the expert witness in direct examination, statements contained in published treatises, periodicals, or pamphlets on a subject of history, medicine, or other science or art, established as a reliable authority by the testimony or admission of the witness or by other expert testimony or by judicial notice. If admitted, the statements may be read into evidence but may not be received as exhibits.

(19) Reputation Concerning Personal or Family History. Reputation among members of a person's family by blood, adoption, or marriage, or among a person's associates, or in the community, concerning a person's birth, adoption, marriage, divorce, death, legitimacy, relationship by blood, adoption, or marriage, ancestry, or other similar fact of personal or family history.

(20) Reputation Concerning Boundaries or General History. Reputation in a community, arising before the controversy, as to boundaries of or customs affecting lands in the community, and reputation as to events of general history important to the community or State or nation in which located.

(21) Reputation as to Character. Reputation of a person's character among associates or in the community.

(22) Judgment of Previous Conviction. Evidence of a final judgment, entered after a trial or upon a plea of guilty (but not upon a plea of nolo contendere), adjudging a person guilty of a crime punishable by death or imprisonment in excess of one year, to prove any fact essential to sustain the judgment, but not including, when offered by the Government in a criminal prosecution for purposes other than impeachment, judgments against persons other than the accused. The pendency of an appeal may be shown but does not affect admissibility.

(23) Judgment as to Personal, Family, or General History, or Boundaries. Judgments as proof of matters of personal, family or general history, or boundaries, essential to the judgment, if the same would be provable by evidence of reputation.

(24) Other Exceptions. A statement not specifically covered by any of the foregoing exceptions but having equivalent circumstantial guarantees of trustworthiness, if the court determines that (A) the statement is offered as evidence of a material fact; (B) the statement is more probative on the point for which it is offered than any other evidence which the proponent can procure through reasonable efforts; and (C) the general purposes of these rules and the interests of justice will best be served by admission of the statement into evidence. However, a statement may not be admitted under this exception unless the proponent of it makes known to the adverse party sufficiently in advance of the trial or hearing to provide the adverse party with a fair opportunity to prepare to meet it, the proponent's intention to offer the statement and the particulars of it, including the name and address of the declarant.

(Amended by Pub.L. 94-149, § 1(11), Dec. 12, 1975, 89 Stat. 805; amended March 2, 1987, eff. Oct. 1, 1987.)

RULE 804. HEARSAY EXCEPTIONS; DECLARANT UNAVAILABLE

(a) Definition of Unavailability. "Unavailability as a witness" includes situations in which the declarant—

(1) is exempted by ruling of the court on the ground of privilege from testifying concerning the subject matter of the declarant's statement; or

(2) persists in refusing to testify concerning the subject matter of the declarant's statement despite an order of the court to do so; or

(3) testifies to a lack of memory of the subject matter of the declarant's statement; or

(4) is unable to be present or to testify at the hearing because of death or then existing physical or mental illness or infirmity; or

(5) is absent from the hearing and the proponent of a statement has been unable to procure the declarant's attendance (or in the case of a hearsay exception under subdivision (b)(2), (3), or (4), the declarant's attendance or testimony) by process or other reasonable means.

A declarant is not unavailable as a witness if his exemption, refusal, claim of lack of memory, inability, or absence is due to the procurement or wrongdoing of the proponent of a statement for the purpose of preventing the witness from attending or testifying.

(b) Hearsay Exceptions. The following are not excluded by the hearsay rule if the declarant is unavailable as a witness:

(1) *Former Testimony.* Testimony given as a witness at another hearing of the same or a different proceeding, or in a deposition taken in compliance with law in the course of the same or another proceeding, if the party against whom the testimony is now offered, or, in a civil action or proceeding, a predecessor in interest, had an opportunity and similar motive to develop the testimony by direct, cross, or redirect examination.

(2) *Statement Under Belief of Impending Death.* In a prosecution for homicide or in a civil action or proceeding, a statement made by a declarant while believing that the declarant's death was imminent, concerning the cause or circumstances of what the declarant believed to be impending death.

(3) *Statement Against Interest.* A statement which was at the time of its making so far contrary to the declarant's pecuniary or proprietary interest, or so far tended to subject the declarant to civil or criminal liability, or to render invalid a claim by the declarant against another, that a reasonable person in the declarant's position would not have made the statement unless believing it to be true. A statement tending to expose the declarant to criminal liability and offered to exculpate the accused is not admissible unless corroborating circumstances clearly indicate the trustworthiness of the statement.

(4) *Statement of Personal or Family History.*

(A) A statement concerning the declarant's own birth, adoption, marriage, divorce, legitimacy, relationship by blood, adoption, or marriage, ancestry, or other similar fact of personal or family history, even though declarant had no means of acquiring personal knowledge of the matter stated; or

(B) a statement concerning the foregoing matters, and death also, of another person, if the declarant was related to the other by blood, adoption, or marriage or was so intimately associated with the other's family as to be likely to have accurate information concerning the matter declared.

(5) *Other Exceptions.* A statement not specifically covered by any of the foregoing exceptions but having equivalent circumstantial guarantees of trustworthiness, if the court determines that (A) the statement is offered as evidence of a material fact; (B) the statement is more probative on the point for which it is offered than any other evidence which the proponent can procure through reasonable efforts; and (C) the general purposes of these rules and the interests of justice will best be served by admission of the statement into evidence. However, a statement may not be admitted under this exception unless the proponent of it makes known to the adverse party sufficiently in advance of the trial or hearing to provide the adverse party with a fair opportunity to prepare to meet it, the proponent's intention to offer the statement and the particulars of it, including the name and address of the declarant.

(Amended by Pub.L. 94-149, § 1(12), (13), Dec. 12, 1975, 89 Stat. 806; amended March 2, 1987, eff. Oct. 1, 1987; amended eff. Nov. 18, 1988.)

APPENDIX II

Expert Witness Resources

BROKERAGE FIRMS

Association of Trial Lawyers of America
1050 31st Street, NW
Washington, DC 20007
(202) 965-3500

Offers database information to attorneys regarding concluded cases, so members may contact each other regarding the performance of expert witnesses.

Consultation Networks, Inc.
1835 K Street, NW
Washington, DC 20006
(202) 775-1747

Offers experts in the physical sciences.

Technical Advisory Service for Attorneys
Headquarters:
1166 DeKalb Pike
Blue Bell, PA 19422-1844
215-275-8272 FAX: 215-275-5577 1-800-523-2319
A Division of Technical Advisory Service, Inc.
(215) 275-8272

Offers databasc information on more than 12,500 experts in over 4,000 categories.

MEDICAL SPECIALISTS

DJS Enterprises
P.O. Box 45437
Los Angeles, CA 90045
(213) 641-6770

Offers database information on physicians who have testified against plaintiffs in personal injury cases.

Medi-Legal Services
531 N. Magnolia Avenue
El Cajon, CA 92020
(619) 579-2135

Private consultancy on medical issues.

Index